A 12-Step Approach
to the Spiritual Exercises
of St. Ignatius

A 12-Step Approach to the Spiritual Exercises of St. Ignatius

Jim Harbaugh, S.J.

SHEED & WARD

Lanham, Chicago, New York, Oxford

Published by Sheed & Ward
An imprint of Rowman & Littlefield Publishers, Inc.
A wholly owned subsidiary of The Rowman & Littlefield Publishing Group, Inc.
4501 Forbes Boulevard, Suite 200
Lanham, MD 20706

PO Box 317
Oxford
OX2 9RU, UK

Distributed by National Book Network

Library of Congress Cataloging-in-Publication Data

Harbaugh, Jim, 1945–
    A 12-step approach to the spiritual exercises of St. Ignatius / Jim Harbaugh.
      p. cm.
    ISBN 1-58051-008-6 (alk. paper)
    ISBN: 978-1-58051-008-0

    1. Spiritual exercises. 2. Ignatius, of Loyola, Saint, 1491–1556. Exercita spiritualia. 3.
Twelve-step programs—Religious aspects—Christianity—Meditations. I. Title.
BV4832.2.H287 1997
248.3—dc21   97-42920
                                                                    CIP

Printed in the United States of America.

Contents

Dedication:

In affection and gratitude, this book is dedicated to Tom Weston, S.J. – friend, mentor, Jesuit brother.

✙

Epigraph

Father Eddie Dowling, S.J., was "the first to note how closely in principle the Twelve Steps of Alcoholics Anonymous paralleled a part of the Exercises of St. Ignatius, a basic spiritual discipline of the Jesuit order" (Bill Wilson at the A.A. 1955 convention in St. Louis, printed in *A.A. Comes of Age*, 37).

"*Spiritual Exercises* which have as their purpose the conquest of self and the regulation of one's life in such a way that no decision is made under the influence of any inordinate attachment" (SE #21, 11).

✤

Acknowledgements

Unless specified otherwise, Scripture excerpts are taken from the *New American Bible* Copyright© 1970 Confraternity of Christian Doctrine, Inc. Washington, DC. Used with permission. All Rights Reserved. No part of the *New American Bible* may be reproduced or transmitted in any form or by any means, electronic or mechanical, including photocopying, recording, or by an information storage and retrieval system, without permission in writing from the copyright owner.

I am also using the following 12 Step literature, all published by Alcoholics Anonymous World Services, Inc., New York:

Alcoholics Anonymous, a.k.a. The Big Book, 3rd ed. (1976), abbreviated BB.

Twelve Steps and Twelve Traditions (19S3), abbreviated 12 X 12.

Alcoholics Anonymous Comes of Age (1957), abbreviated AACA.

As Bill Sees It (1967), abbreviated ABSI.

This material is reprinted with the permission of Alcoholics Anonymous World Services, Inc. Permission to reprint this material does not mean that A. A. has reviewed or approved the contents of this publication. A. A. is a program of recovery from alcoholism *only* –

use of this material in any other non-A. A. context, does not imply otherwise.

Additionally, although A. A. is a spiritual program, it is not a religious program. Hence, A. A. is not allied with any sect, denomination or specific spiritual belief.

In addition, I have found the following works helpful in writing about the Jewish and the Christian Scriptures:

Raymond Brown, S.S., Joseph Fitzmyer, S.J., and Roland E. Murphy, O. Carm., eds. *The Jerome Biblical Commentary.* Englewood Cliffs, NJ: Prentice-Hall, 1968.

_____. *The New Jerome Biblical Commentary.* Englewood Cliffs, NJ: Prentice-Hall, 1990.

John Dominic Crossan. *Jesus: A Revolutionary Biography.* San Francisco: HarperCollins, 1994.

J. C. Fenton. *The Gospel of St. Matthew.* London: Penguin Books, 1963.

Reginald H. Fuller. *Preaching the New Lectionary: The Word of God for the Church Today.* Collegeville, MN: Liturgical Press, 1974.

Eugene LaVerdiere, S.S.S. *Luke.* Wilmington, Delaware: Michael Glazier, 1980.

D. E. Nineham. *The Gospel of St. Mark.* London: Penguin Books, 1969.

George V. Wigram and Ralph D. Winter. *The Word Study Concordance.* Wheaton, IL: Tyndale House, 1978.

The following reference books on A. A. literature and history were also very helpful:

Alcoholics Anonymous World Services, Inc. *Dr. Bob and the Good Oldtimers: A Biography, with Recollections of Early A. A. in the Midwest.* New York, 1980.

_____. *Pass It On: The Story of Bill Wilson and How the A. A. Message Reached the World.* New York, 1984.

Stewart C. *A Reference Guide to the Big Book of Alcoholics Anonymous.* Seattle: Recovery Press, 1986.

Ernie Kurtz. *Not-God: A History of Alcoholics Anonymous.* Center City, Minnesota: Hazelden, 1979.

In particular, I have quoted or paraphrased material from the following sources (permission has been given where copyrighted material is directly quoted):

William James. *The Varieties of Religious Experience: A Study in Human Nature.* 1902; rpt. New York: MacMillan, 1961.

Ernest Kurtz and Katherine Ketcham. *The Spirituality of Imperfection: Modern Wisdom from Classic Stories.* New York: Bantam, 1992.

Gerald May. *Addiction and Grace.* San Francisco: HarperCollins, 1991.

Songs: Joan Osbourne, "One of Us"

Joni Mitchell, "Woodstock"

Finally, these are some works I have used frequently in commenting on the Spiritual Exercises of St. Ignatius of Loyola:

Text: Unless otherwise specified, I am quoting from Fr. Louis Puhl's translation of the Spiritual Exercises – Westminster, MD: Newman Press, 1959. I have also found helpful these works on Ignatian spirituality:

William A. Barry, S.J. *Finding God in All Things: A Companion to The Spiritual Exercises.* Notre Dame, IN: Ave Maria Press, 1991.

Ignatius of Loyola. *Spiritual Exercises and Selected Works.* George Ganss, S.J., et al., eds. and trans. New York: Paulist Press, 1991. Quoted with permission.

✛

Introduction

The Background: Ignatius and Bill W.

In *A.A. Comes of Age*, Bill Wilson, the co-founder of Alcoholics Anonymous, describes his first meeting with Eddie Dowling. At first Bill thought he was "some bum . . . from St. Louis," but he later turned out to be a Jesuit priest. Fr. Dowling had traveled all the way to New York City to find Bill, on a winter night of rain and sleet. The priest, though not an alcoholic himself, had helped get the first A.A. group in St. Louis (my home town) started. He was excited by resemblances he thought he saw between the A.A. 12 Step approach and the Spiritual Exercises of St. Ignatius of Loyola, the founder of the Jesuits (whose official name is, by the way, "Society of Jesus").

Bill found Dowling inspiring. The priest had "the most remarkable pair of eyes I have ever seen," meeting him was "a moving and mysterious experience," and during his long friendship with Bill, Fr. Dowling "always brought to me the same sense of grace and the presence of God" (AACA, 38). But Bill W. doesn't say whether he agreed with Dowling on the resemblance between the 12 Steps and the Spiritual Exercises, nor does he say anything about the life of St. Ignatius. I wonder if Bill ever heard the full story of the man who founded the Jesuits. If he had, he might have been struck by certain resemblances to his own "personal adventures before and after" [recovery] (BB, 58).

Like Bill, Ignatius of Loyola was not a particularly religious person until well into mid-life – rather, they were both "worldly indeed" (BB, 50). In their thirties, both of them hit a personal bottom. Bill was wiped out financially by the '29 stock market crash and then, largely unemployable, proceeded to drink his way in and out of hospitals for several years, living on the salary of his wife, Lois. At a battle in Pamplona, Spain, Ignatius suffered a serious leg injury, which required a long rehabilitation, longer in fact because Ignatius wanted two good legs for what he presumed would be his career as a soldier-courtier. In each case, personal bottom led to a dramatic change of life-course. Bill, on the verge of institutionalization for alcoholism, was contacted by an old drinking buddy, now sobered by his contact with a Christian organization; Ignatius was given only a life of Jesus and a book of saints' lives to read during his convalescence.

Inspired by the spiritual recovery of his old crony, Bill revisited a hospital at which he had been a patient more than once, in order to detox; while withdrawing medically from alcohol, he had a mystical experience – he said that his room filled with light – after which he never drank again. Ignatius' experience was of "the educational variety" (BB, 569). In the course of his reading, he thought about his future. And he was self-reflective enough to notice that when he thought about continuing as he had been, he felt good for a while but then felt flat. But when he thought of emulating people who had followed Jesus in a noteworthy way, he felt good, *and he kept feeling good.*

Both men made a lot of mistakes in the early days after their conversions, with the fervent wrong-headedness typical of spiritual rookies (in A.A. this is called the Pink Cloud phase). Bill tried to tell other alcoholics about his

xiv   *A 12-Step Approach to the Spiritual Exercises of St. Ignatius*

spiritual experience; but none of them wanted to hear about it. Ignatius wanted to become a Great Saint in a real hurry, but instead drove himself crazy with fasting and sleep-deprivation and living in a cave.

Both were eventually brought around by their contact with a good listener. Six months sober, Bill went on a disastrous business trip to Akron (Bill was a New Yorker); near relapsing, he instead got the name of an alcoholic from a local clergyman. That alcoholic, Dr. Bob Smith, met with Bill, who had now decided to tell his story to alcoholic prospects rather than preach to them. This new approach worked; and the two became the nucleus of Alcoholics Anonymous.

Ignatius, after coming close to suicide because of his ferocious spiritual regimen, consulted a spiritual director, who brought him back down to earth and helped him to rejoin the human race. After a few more attempts to find an "easier, softer [and quicker] way" (BB, 58) to become a saint, he decided to do some slow, painstaking footwork: he went back to school and began the years-long process that would prepare him for Catholic priesthood. While in college, he met some young men (to whom he would have seemed a grizzled veteran), and, like Bill, told them his spiritual story. They wanted what he had, and were willing to go to considerable lengths to get it, so they did what he had done, and got similar spiritual results. Eventually they decided to commit themselves to service work, which by fits and starts and false moves led in time to the formation of the Society of Jesus – the Jesuits.

So the stories of Bill and Ignatius do have a lot in common. And so do the core documents that reflect their experience. After a few years of working successfully with other alcoholics, Bill wrote down the methods that had helped him and his companions to apply "spiritual principles" to recovery from alcoholism; in time, and out of several possibilities, the resulting book was called *Alcoholics Anonymous,* published in 1939. (The book gave the movement its name, not the other way around.) The first chapter was Bill's story. Likewise Ignatius, after some years of passing on to his friends his insights into prayer, pulled his notes together and produced a book called the *Spiritual Exercises.* Unlike Bill, Ignatius included no autobiographical material; but he did later dictate some autobiographical notes to his secretary.

So we are back to Eddie Dowling's notion, which he traveled all the way from St. Louis to New York in December to share with Bill W.: given that the biographies of Ignatius and Bill were similar, what about the principles in their books? Was Dowling right to see a resemblance there?

In terms of some core ideas, I think he was. Central both to "the 12 Step approach" and to the *Spiritual Exercises* is the notion that what is most needed if a human being wants to move from misery to contentment is a thorough conversion. The "Big Book" (the nickname for *Alcoholics Anonymous,* derived from the absurdly thick paper on which it was first printed), invoking no less a personage than Carl Jung, defines conversion as "vital spiritual experiences," or "an entire psychic change" (27, xxvii). Ignatius, looking more to its effects than to its essence, defines conversion as getting free from "inordinate attachments."

Both Bill and Ignatius believe that conversion can be evoked, or facilitated, by a methodical, highly structured approach; indeed, both approaches have been criticized for being too regimented. Both the *Spiritual Exercises* and *Alcoholics Anonymous* assume that conversion begins with a deep sense of human brokenness (Ignatius' "First Week" and Bill's First Step). Both move next to a sense of God's healing power. Inspirited by this power, the recovering person, or the person making the Spiritual Exercises, makes a "searching and fearless moral inventory" (Step Four); this is shared with another person. (Both Bill and Ignatius came over time to see the importance of having a spiritual guide, or a "sponsor" in 12 Step lingo; Eddie Dowling played precisely this role in Bill's life).

In both approaches, the person goes on to live a life that involves "prayer and meditation," as well as efforts to improve the conscious contact with God initiated or refurbished at the time of conversion (see Step Eleven in A.A.). And the person is urged to keep their conversion alive by service of others (Step Twelve; cf. the material on choice – "election" – of a way of life in the *Exercises*).

However, there are also big differences between Bill's approach and Ignatius'. Perhaps the most obvious is the profound importance of Jesus in the *Exercises*; they are divided into Four Weeks, and all but the First focus almost entirely on events in the life of Christ. By contrast, Bill decided early on to cut the connection between his embryonic group of recovered alcoholics and the Christian group within which it had begun. When *Alcoholics Anonymous* came out, prospective members were told that they could regard their spiritual experiences in any way that made sense to them – it was to be God as they understood God. Atheist and agnostic members were welcome. Despite Bill's debt to the thought of William James (see BB, 28), A.A. puts a primacy on "spiritual," not "religious," experiences.

This suggests another big difference between the two approaches. Ignatius has a strong sense of the Catholic Church at the horizon of the retreatant's world, and even includes "Rules for Thinking with the Church." A.A., by contrast, goes out of its way to avoid enforcing any kind of orthodoxy: the first draft of the Big Book was deliberately revised to replace statements like "You must do this" with "This is what we did." To cite one important instance, the Steps, which "we [recovering alcoholics] took," are only "suggested" (BB, 59).

But perhaps this second difference is not so sharp as it at first appears. It took Ignatius many years to realize the importance of a larger believing community; at first he was all too much a rugged spiritual individualist, and even fell afoul of the Spanish Inquisition, early in his college career. By the same token, Bill came in time, to realize that something more than just the individual's conversion by means of the 12 Steps was required: in 1950, at his suggestion, A.A. adopted the Twelve Traditions, shaping relations within and between A.A. groups, at its first International Convention (see Meditation 52, below).

The Traditions are not rules, of course; they are rather ideals for a society in which love is the only law. But I think Ignatius would have found them congenial, and above all in their thoroughgoing insistence on radical poverty – there is to be no "money, property, [or] prestige" in A.A. (Tradition Six). It's no accident, by the way, that when Bill cites a prayer in his commentary on Step Eleven, he invokes the prayer of St. Francis, the lover of Lady Poverty, "Make me an instrument of your peace" (in the 12 X 12, i.e., *Twelve Steps and Twelve Traditions*, Bill's 1953 Talmudic commentary on the Big Book)

In any event, despite the differences between the 12 Steps and the *Spiritual Exercises*, Bill found Eddie Dowling's spiritual direction profoundly helpful for the rest of Dowling's life, which went on for twenty years after their first meeting. Yet Bill never joined the Catholic Church and Eddie Dowling never joined A.A. There was enough common ground for them even so.

What I want to do in this book is not so much study the extent of that common ground, much less argue that it is there. Rather, I am going to assume it's there, and build something on it. My assumption here is that a lot of recovering people may find that the spiritual path they have begun with the Twelve Steps leads to other, sometimes surprising paths – any self-respecting spiritual path ought to. It may even lead them to want to explore the path Ignatius stumbled on almost five hundred years ago. Some of the scenery will seem decidedly familiar. In the same way, people who have made the Spiritual Exercises may subsequently find they need the Twelve Steps. They too may feel curiously at home in the world of the Recovering.

II: Some Ways to Use This Book

Practically, I would suggest that the best way to use this book is to get a spiritual guide who will agree to walk this path with you. You may already have one; in that case you need only have them read along with you. It would help if they know both 12 Step and Ignatian lingo, but what matters most is that they know *you* and that they be people who pray themselves. One nuance: Ignatius meant for only the director (the "sponsor," to use the 12 Step term) to have a copy of the *Exercises,* but I want both directors and directees to have copies of this book, perhaps because I have never liked surprises.

For that matter, I guess you could pray through this book on your own, and perhaps many people who use it will do it that way. But promise me at least that you'll tell your sponsor, or some other confidant, what you're up to. We travel any path better if we travel together.

I have broken up the material of the *Exercises* into 52 meditations – with an obvious eye to having someone spend a year going through this book, one meditation a week (Bill and Ignatius aren't the only anal, methodical students of spirituality). Of course, please follow the Ignatian principle of pausing where you find fruit; there are no penalties assessed for taking more or less than a year.

More specifically, you may want to work through the book, alone or with a director, by reading one of my Meditations, including any Scripture citations, on Sunday, before or after church (if you attend one), or on another regular day of the week if you prefer. During the rest of the week you can glance at the whole Meditation again, or ponder again a passage you've highlighted because it particularly struck you. You will want to see your director, if you have one, regularly, say, once a month. I have inserted reminders of this in the Meditations themselves, particularly at important transitions.

During your actual periods of meditation – your "Eleventh Step work," in 12-Step language – you might want to go about it in an orderly way. Bill W. liked to give "definite and valuable suggestions" about "prayer and meditation" (see BB, 86, 85). For example, in the 12 X 12 (99-102), he offers some specific suggestions about how to pray your way through the Peace Prayer of St. Francis of Assisi.

For his part, Ignatius also offers a lot of "definite . . . suggestions" about how to pray. For instance, the retreatant may begin by reciting a familiar prayer, just as many 12-Step meetings begin with the Serenity Prayer. Then the retreatant gets more into the mood for meditation by using a couple of preparatory thoughts, which he calls "preludes" (*preambulos* in Spanish: essentially a warm up before a spiritual run).

Often the First Prelude is the Big Picture of the particular Meditation. In some cases, where Ignatius offers a scene for us to contemplate, we may literally want to imagine a large, living tableau of the scene. When we're pondering something more abstract, we may nevertheless want to use our imaginations – even our physical senses – to come up with concrete metaphors for the concept (see SE #47).

The Second Prelude is usually "to ask God for what I desire" from this particular Meditation. This may be deeper intellectual understanding, or a particular appropriate feeling, or greater clarity about God's will. For our fast-food age, I have subjoined to each Meditation a kind of Second Prelude, which briefly sums up the main point of that Meditation in the form of a brief prayer. I call them "Second Preludes, to Go." You can use them to come back to attention if your mind wanders during your period of prayer. You can also use them in the course of the week to remind you of what you're praying over at this point.

After these preliminaries, the retreatant is to consider the material provided in the meditation. Here it's important to know what kind of praying works best for you, and this is yet another area where having a director can be very helpful. Some people are imaginative; some are cognitive. Some are feelers; some are thinkers. Some have a strong pictorial sense; others (like me) are more verbal, more auditory. Some need to sit quietly; some need to move around or do things with their hands. Some like prayer that empties them; others like prayer that fills them.

The point is to find, or continue, the way of meditating that works best for you. "Works" in this context means above all "increases your ability to know and to do God's will for you"; dazzling insights and thrilling emotions are nice, but dull and bland can be just fine if they help you to serve people more lovingly.

In any case, toward the end of the time you have decided to set aside for meditation, Ignatius suggests you spend some time conversing with God, from whatever place your Meditation has taken you, whether that place seems relevant to the Topic of the Meditation for that week or not. You may want to end your period of meditation with another familiar prayer, for instance, the Lord's Prayer (again, many meetings close this way). Finally, Ignatius suggests writing (or drawing, if you like) after or even during your prayer time, partly by way of keeping a spiritual journal.

Another way to go through this book would be to form a prayer or study group. On whatever evening or morning of the week your group gathers, you can read, discuss, or pray over the Meditation for that week. The group, perhaps with the aid of a facilitator, could direct itself. For example, your group may want to use the 12-Step method of "taking a group conscience" to determine when to pause and when to move on in the Meditations and in the "Four Weeks" into which Ignatius divided them.

In addition, people who do a lot of spiritual directing or who give retreats may want to swipe an idea here or there from this book. That's fine. I deeply believe that 12 Step people and church people (and many of us are both) have a wealth of information to exchange, and I would love this book to serve as a vehicle, or even just as a conversational icebreaker ("It *can't* be as simple as he says it is!").

My method all through this book, as in other books of mine, will be to begin with the older text, the *Exercises,* and to translate that little by little into 12 Step language. As with any translation, this can serve to jolt even someone who knows the older version into a fresh appreciation of that text. And newcomers to recovery can come to see that very ancient wisdom is just as relevant to them and their struggles as it was when it was first discerned. This is the point of Ernie Kurtz's splendid *Spirituality of Imperfection*: in coming up with the 12 Steps, A.A. half-accidentally tapped into a vein of spiritual wisdom that had been around for millennia. The *Spiritual Exercises* are a seam in that vein. Dig in.

Two Beloved Prayers

Let's begin this spiritual journey with two prayers: One prefaces the *Exercises*; the other has been a 12 Step favorite since shortly after it was crafted by the great American Protestant theologian Reinhold Niebuhr.

Reflection on the Anima Christi

> Soul of Christ, sanctify me;
> Body of Christ, save me;
> Blood of Christ, inebriate me.
> Water from the side of Christ, wash me.
> Passion of Christ, strengthen me.
> O Good Jesus, hear me.
> Within your wounds hide me.
> Never permit me to be separated from you.
> From evil deliver me.
> In the hour of my death call me.
> And bid me come to you,
> That, with the saints, I may praise you,
> forever and ever. Amen.

Comment: This ancient prayer may seem a little odd at first. Oddest of all, perhaps, is that the person saying the prayer asks to be made drunk on Jesus' blood. This may sound ghoulish, or sordid.

But I think Bill W. was right when he noted that alcoholics were looking for some kind of transcendent experience, at least at the beginning of their drinking (see *As*

Bill Sees It, #323). Human beings have wanted for millennia to attain altered states, to expand consciousness, and drugs are one way to do this – a way, as it happens, with too many undesirable side effects, particularly over the long haul. But the principle is sound: we want to be intoxicated in the sense of being able to let go of our niggling little egos, our fears and resentments and narrow-mindedness. We want to have some sense of the great realities all around us.

In Christian services, wine – a mind-altering substance – serves as a powerful sign of Christ's blood. Over the wine we say Jesus' words from the Last Supper, when he said the wine was a new covenant in his blood. But when Jesus said the bread was his body, and the wine was his blood, he meant that he was giving all of himself to us. "How shall I make a return to the Lord for all the good the Lord has done for me?" (Ps. 116:12). We can give ourselves back (see the Contemplation to Get the Love of God, #49-50, below).

So what we are asking for in the *Anima Christi* is to be taken out of ourselves by being filled up with Christ's spirit, Christ's consciousness, Christ's loving way of looking at people and the world. The rest of this prayer makes the same point. While you are using this book of meditations, pray this prayer often, asking that you may get "high" by praying over your relationship with the God of Jesus, a God who calls to a change of heart and to service.

Reflection on the Serenity Prayer

> God, grant me the serenity
> to accept the things I cannot change;
> courage to change the things I can;
> and the wisdom to know the difference.

Comment: It's a good preparation for the 12 Steps, and for the Spiritual Exercises, to reflect on this prayer, since, as we will soon see, the purpose of both is precisely to help us attain wisdom. People take up the 12 Steps largely because they have been throwing will-power at things and people over which in fact they have no control – alcohol and alcoholics, to name two. They have been trying to change things they cannot really change. So the first part of the prayer comes as news – and relief: some things are meant to be accepted, with as much serenity as we can muster, grudgingly or gratefully.

But compulsive people go to extremes, and so we may at first figure that we need to accept everything, just as we used to try to change everything. But it's not that simple – some things we *can* change, *ought* to change. Above all we must change our attitudes and our hearts (a change of heart is a conversion – *metanoia* in the Gospels). But when to change, when to accept? The prayer climaxes with a request for the wisdom to know when, for that is what we need above all.

During the time you are using this book, please ask your Higher Power for wisdom every day. We need God's help to know, in Bob Seger's words, "what to leave in/ what to leave out" of our lives.

Meditation 1

Title and Purpose of the Exercises

"SPIRITUAL EXERCISES which *have as their purpose the conquest of self and the regulation of one's life* in such a way that no decision is made under the influence of any inordinate attachment" (SE, #21).

This week let's begin our preparations for the Exercises proper with some reflections on the long form of the title for these notes of Ignatius' about his spiritual path. Why would anyone, and especially an alcoholic, set out on this path in the first place, since it will involve considerable work? "[T]he conquest of self and the regulation of one's life" don't sound very inviting. As Bill notes, "the average alcoholic, self-centered in the extreme, doesn't care for [such a] prospect" (12 X 12, 24).

However, an alcoholic who wants to recover will have to adopt just such "attitudes and actions . . . in order to stay alive" (12 X 12, 24). My favorite passage in the Big Book, which comes right after the Steps, argues that underneath all the bizarre and/or dreary behavior of addicts and the people who care about them is "the root of our troubles": "selfishness, self-centeredness" (BB, 62). If we are going to make good our recovery from alcoholism, we "must be rid of this selfishness. . . . And there often seems no way of entirely getting rid of self without [God's] aid" (BB, 62). So the Exercises and the 12 Steps have the same end in view: "the conquest of self," which necessarily requires the help of "a Power greater than [ourselves]" (BB, 45).

4

Of course, the word "conquest" here may evoke a little glamour – maybe we think of the kind of knightly figures on horseback who peopled the medieval romances of which St. Ignatius was so fond before his conversion (they were his version of Bill's alcoholic fantasy of being a financial Napoleon [see BB, 4]). But "the regulation of one's life" sounds hopelessly drab, except possibly to engineers or mechanics. Alcoholics want a little dash, a bit of color – not somebody tinkering cautiously with a thermostat.

Yet what we alcoholics want is not what we need, in this case as in so many others. We may not like it, but the fact – painfully apparent to others, rarely to us – is that "[w]e alcoholics are undisciplined" (BB, 88). Some "regulation" – playing by the rules, etymologically – is what we really need. The good news is that this discipline need not be administered by another, fallible human being, and not even by ourselves – as alcoholics, we would probably veer from one extreme to the other. No, this regulation will be provided by "a loving God" (Tradition Two): "we let God discipline us" (BB, 88). During this first week of our journey, let us ask that God will give us the wisdom to want to get over ourselves – or at least to "want to want to" (see BB, 109).

Second Prelude, to Go: Dear God, give me the desire to get over myself so I can become myself.

Meditation 2

More on the Purpose of the Exercises

"SPIRITUAL EXERCISES which have as their purpose the conquest of self and the regulation of one's life in such a way that *no decision is made under the influence of any inordinate attachment.*"

This week I want to concentrate on the second half of Ignatius' prefatory statement. If with God's help we do get our lives conquered and regulated, what will we do with our better-regulated lives? A 12 Step answer would be "carry the message" and "practice these principles in all our affairs" (Step 12). In Ignatian terms, we know we have undergone "deep and effective spiritual experiences" (BB, 25) if we choose to live our lives in the way that we think gives best service to God and to other human beings. The "decisions" we come to after a powerful experience of prayer like the Exercises are decisions about large, even about once-in-a-lifetime, matters: What is our life-calling? With whom should we spend our lives?

What could stand in the way of our making a good decision in such matters? Ignatius' reply: "The influence of any inordinate attachment." A few years ago, Ignatius's language here might have sounded strange or archaic to the general reader. But thanks to the work of Gerald May, and particularly to his masterful little treatise *Addiction and Grace* (1988), "attachment" is now very much part of the vocabulary of a lot of students of recovery. May uses this old spiritual term interchangeably with the more modern word "addiction." An even older religious term for both is "idolatry." What we are addicted to, or attached to, is anything that we rely on more than we rely on God. And these things are endlessly subtle – May has a very long list of them. Alcohol and other psychoactive substances simply produce some of the more lurid effects, but "attachment" can even take the homely form of an addiction to nasal spray (see A & G, 22-24). Ignatius refines the term by calling them *"inordinate"* (excessive, ill-regulated) attachments, but any attachment can become an addiction.

Attachments have many bad effects – they frequently cost a lot of money, for example, and they're often murder on human relationships. But in the context of the Exercises, what makes attachments so poisonous is that they lead to poor life-choices. For instance, I realized my drinking had become alcoholic, not because of its sheer quantity (although that was a big clue), but because the need to drink entered every daily life-choice I made – where I go, when I go, with whom I go. I was not free, for example, to go anywhere for any length of time if I couldn't smuggle in enough liquor. And all attachments, even less squalid ones like attachments to running, or to one's own ideas, have the same potential to impede generous choices.

It's also a hallmark of attachment/addiction to induce denial of the fact that one is addicted. So let our prayer this week be that during the First Week of the Exercises, which we will be entering soon, we can come to a better sense of our attachments. In time we will be able to "humbly ask God to remove" them (cf. Step Seven), so that we can make freer choices about how we live and love.

Second Prelude, to Go: Dear God, show me this week all the things I'm stuck to and need to get free from to serve you better.

Meditation 3

First Principle and Foundation (Part I)

"Human beings are created to praise, reverence, and serve God our Lord, and by this means to save their souls. The other things on the face of the earth are created for human beings to help them in attaining the end for which they are created. Hence, humans are to make use of them in as far as they help them in the attainment of their end, and they must rid themselves of them in as far as they prove a hindrance to them. Therefore, we must make ourselves indifferent to all created things, as far as we are allowed free choice and are not under any prohibition. Consequently, as far as we are concerned, we should not prefer health to sickness, riches to poverty, honor to dishonor, a long life to a short life. The same holds for other things. Our one desire and choice should be what is more conducive to the end for which we are created" (SE, #23).

St. Ignatius offers this statement as "the first principle" of the Exercises, the logical premise out of which the rest will flow, the foundation stone on which "a wonderfully effective spiritual structure can be built" (BB, 47). In fact, it is a principle well worth "practicing in all our affairs" (Step 12) because what it amounts to is summed up in the wise A.A. slogan "First Things First" (BB, 135).

What comes first for human beings is not "the other things on the face of the earth." As meditation 2 suggested, these other things – good in themselves, or God would not have created them – can be a trap for human beings. This occurs if we make them into our gods, if we become "attached" to them, or "addicted" to them, in such a way that they prevent us from doing what we were really created to do – freely serve God. If we miss this goal, we miss everything – we never do what we came here to do, we never get to be the person we were uniquely designed to be. Addictions – to chemicals or to activities or to people – erode our freedom until we can't be ourselves any more; we have to serve our idols, we have to spend all our time and energy getting our substances and then getting over them the next morning.

How to put God first, then? What St. Ignatius says sounds so straightforward, so relentlessly logical: all we need do is "make use of [creatures] in as far as they help" and "rid [our]selves of them in as far as they prove a hindrance." But how can we addicted people follow this eminently sensible advice, when "lack of power" is "our dilemma" (BB, 45)? For an alcoholic, what must come first is "a Power greater than [ourselves] which will solve [our] problem" (BB, 45), or, in the words of Step Two, a Power that can restore us to sanity. So the First Things for us are two: a Greater Power – St. Ignatius called his "God our Lord" – and the sanity, the sobriety, that that Power brings us when we acknowledge our powerlessness. During this week, let's ponder how fundamental sobriety is to all that we choose and all that we do in our daily lives.

Second Prelude, to Go: Dear God, show me how I am rooted and grounded in your gift of recovery.

Meditation 4

First Principle and Foundation (Part II)

> "Human beings are created to praise, reverence, and serve God our Lord, and by this means to save their souls. The other things on the face of the earth are created for human beings to help them in attaining the end for which they are created. Hence, humans are to make use of them in as far as they help them in the attainment of their end, and they must rid themselves of them in as far as they prove a hindrance to them. *There-fore, we must make ourselves indifferent to all created things, as far as we are allowed free choice and are not under any prohibition. Consequently, as far as we are concerned, we should not prefer health to sickness, riches to poverty, honor to dishonor, a long life to a short life. The same holds for other things. Our one de-sire and choice should be what is more conducive to the end for which we are created*" (SE, #23).

This week we meditate on the second half of the First Principle and Foundation. Last week we concluded that sanity, or sobriety, comes first for alcoholics. And so this week it logically follows that recovering people should do a lot of what helps them stay sober (or abstinent, or healthy in relationships), because these things are "condu-cive to the end for which we are created." And we should avoid things, insofar as we can, that make us want to drink, or gamble, or enter abusive relationships.

Ignatius closes off a couple of loopholes, which might occur to alcoholics a bit faster than they would to other people. The first loophole: I used to drink to relieve job stress; many people do. But it wouldn't make sense for me to claim (much as I might like to on certain days) that work makes me want to drink, so I shouldn't have to work. In some matters we are not "allowed free choice" – adults should meet adult responsibilities and commitments, because these help us to become the people we were created to be. We may want to *change* jobs or relationships, but skipping them altogether is "under . . . prohibition" if we want to be human beings.

The second loophole is more subtle, or at least I found it a problem for a lot of years. What does Ignatius mean by "indifferent"? We shouldn't worship "created things," but surely it's unhealthy not to care whether we're sick or well. And most of us can identify with Sophie Tucker's immortal dictum: "I've been rich and I've been poor. Rich is better."

I think what Ignatius means by "indifference" is similar to what Al-Anon means by "detachment with love." It doesn't mean "not caring," and certainly "not caring in a vindictive or envious spirit." It means caring in an "ordinate" way – caring enough, but not so much that the loss of this person or that job, of health or wealth, will knock us off balance so badly that we will relapse to our addictions. As the Big Book puts it, "Job or no job – wife or no wife – we simply do not stop drinking so long as we place dependence upon other people" – or upon our own notions of how our lives should evolve – "ahead of dependence on God" (BB, 98). Or, more simply, "either God is everything or else [God] is nothing" (BB, 53).

The first time I encountered the First Principle, I was an unusually clueless 17-year-old Jesuit novice. Healthy as a horse, I sat in my little prayer-cell trying to imagine what real "sickness" would be like, staging noble little playlets in my imagination. But the First Principle works better, like a lot of spiritual truths, in retrospect, or when faced with reality. For the last seven years I've had chronic back pain; the First Principle assures me, at 52, that it's still possible for me to serve God as only I will ever be able to serve God, back pain or no back pain. I can be "indifferent" too, "detached" from this unpleasant reality. But it's not easy; I need all the help I can get from a Power greater than myself, usually working through other people.

This week, our prayer should continue to focus on those things we may be attached to. We may in fact have lost them already (like youth), and yet we're even more attached to them. Can we humbly ask God to take them – or to keep them if they're already gone – knowing we can go on without them?

Second Prelude, to Go: Dear God, take anything of mine that keeps me from you and from my fellows. You can have anything that keeps me from being the person you need me to be.

❖

First Week

So far we have been considering the basics, "a group of principles, spiritual in their nature, which, if practiced as a way of life, can . . . enable [a person] to become happily and usefully whole" (12 X 12, Foreword, 15). And we have been trying to view human life as God views it. During the next phase of our spiritual journey, we will take a "searching and fearless" (Step Four) look at the ways in which we have violated these spiritual principles and so caused other people and ourselves unhappiness. This whole next phase – which Ignatius calls the First Week – is about acknowledging the truth of the First Step: we need God's help to manage our lives. On our own we too often make messes of them. As we move from the warm-up exercises of the retreat to the main event, we might want to have a session with whoever is our guide along this way.

Meditation 5

Angels and Sin

"[R]ecall that [the angels] were created in the
state of grace, that they did not want to make use
of the freedom God gave them to reverence and
obey their Creator and Lord, and so falling into
pride, were changed from grace to hatred of
God, and cast out of heaven into hell" (SE, #50)

During the First Week (or, more precisely, First Phase or
First Movement) of the Exercises, St. Ignatius asks us to
begin where the Steps begin – with our powerlessness, our
unmanageability. He uses moral language, as the Big
Book often does: Dr. William Silkworth, the first outside
expert to study A.A., called the 12 Step program "moral
psychology" (BB, xxv). Rather than talking about "serious
violations of moral principles" or an "index of maladjust-
ments" (12 X 12, 48), Ignatius prefers the older, blunter
term "sin." What "sin" adds to "defects of character" or
"violations of moral principles" is the notion of harm
done to a relationship, either with other human beings,
or with creation, or with a Power greater than ourselves.

Ignatius invites us to consider three paradigmatic sins
over this and the next two weeks. This week we are to reflect on the sin of the angels. The whole notion of angels
has made something of a comeback over the last few
years; but not everyone believes in them. For 12 Step purposes, perhaps we can use the notion of "angels as you
understand angels." In the Biblical stories on which Ignatius is drawing, angels are powerful beings whose primary
purpose is to carry very personal messages from God to

particular individuals – frequently messages about life choices, the focus of the Exercises. (Some people, in fact, understand "angels" as vivid encounters with the Higher Power rather than as separate beings.)

Specifically, Ignatius refers to a story pieced together from some rather obscure passages of the Bible, more familiar perhaps to us through the first part of Milton's epic *Paradise Lost*, written a hundred years after Ignatius' time. Ignatius summarizes that story, and it turns out to be about a misuse of "freedom," a misuse that could be characterized as "self-will run riot" (BB, 62).

The First Principle and Foundation for angels is the same as for human beings: they ought to choose to become the beings they were created to be, acknowledging that they didn't make themselves. One concept of angels is that they are pure spirit, absolutely simple, so their "attachment," their "addiction," was correspondingly simple. They went right to the heart of the matter, and fell "into pride": some of them, so the story goes, chose their own will rather than God's, chose to act as if they were their own Higher Power.

This is relevant for human beings, for, as Bill W. notes, "pride heads the procession" of "major human failings" (12 X 12, 48). Or, as the Big Book puts it, "self-centeredness . . . is the root of all our troubles" (62). When we choose things, rather than choosing God, it is ultimately our own wills that we are worshipping.

The point here, then, is not speculation about those angels who fell from grace. Rather, Ignatius wants us to use their story to understand more deeply the process by which we fall from grace, become attached to things. The idea of hating God, of being "cast out of heaven into hell," might seem over-inflated or melodramatic to some people, but addicts may find this notion squares with their experience.

To be in the throes of an addiction is frequently compared by recovering addicts to a trip to hell. And it is impossible to have two masters, as Jesus noted (Lk 16:13); if you love one – the one to which you are addicted – you have to hate the other, even if the other is God.

So angels and drunks turn out to have a lot in common. Drunks often want to be like angels, having "glimpses of the Absolute and a heightened feeling of identification with the cosmos" (ABSI, #323). As with the angels, this lust for transcendent experience leads in addicts to pride and a great fall from grace: from ease into dis-ease. But – lucky for us – here the resemblance ends. Since angels are so simple, the thinking goes, anything they decide is irreversible. Not so human beings: the whole point of the house-cleaning the Steps prescribe is to help us to change our minds, and to make amends for our misbehavior. For human beings, and especially for addicted human beings, there is a way back from hell.

Second Prelude, to Go: Dear God, help me always to choose what you want rather than what I want. And help me to see that you want better things for me than I want.

Meditation 6

The First People and Sin

(See SE, #51)

In this week's meditation, we come down to earth – literally. Angels are not human beings, luckily for us. This week's meditation focuses on human beings, and specifically the first two, the prototypes, who, as the book of Genesis relates, were formed from the soil. What's the meaning of the story of Adam and Eve, the first members of the human family to have to deal with desire and limitation?

For our purposes, what matters most is not apples or trees or gardens. The point for recovering people of the story of Adam and Eve is that they wanted to have the same kind of power as a power greater than themselves had. They wanted to do their will – "self-will run riot" again – rather than God's will. In short, they refused to take the Third Step; rather than have someone else guide their will and their lives, they wanted to be "like gods" (Gen 3:5). They wanted to be the ones to decide what went into their mouths.

Addiction is a disease of will-power. Addicts are obsessed with the notion that "[o]ur human resources, marshaled by the will," ought to be "sufficient" (BB, 45) – sufficient to master alcohol or anything else. It is in this "obsession" – an "obsession" shared, ironically, by "every abnormal drinker" (BB, 30) – that addicts are the daughters and sons of Adam and Eve.

17

As with the sin of our cousins the angels, this human willfulness is a kind of pride. And it leads to similarly bleak results: instead of the paradise God had in mind, the earth is a place where families struggle to survive. In fact, the greatest dangers to family members may come from their kin – one of the first human children kills his brother, because Cain, like any addict, does not believe there is enough of something, God's love specifically, for him and for anybody else.

To summarize: from the beginning human beings have been torn, inside and outside, by fear and self-will and resentment and the need to control. "Above everything, we alcoholics must be rid of this selfishness" (BB, 62). But how on earth can we step outside of our ancient family heritage of violence? As we shall see the week after next, we are empowered to do this by a descendant of Adam and Eve, a human brother, who is also a power greater than ourselves: "[T]hanks be to God who has given us the victory through our Lord Jesus Christ" (1 Cor 15:57).

Second Prelude, to Go: Dear God, relieve me of the bondage of self that I may better do thy will (from the Third Step Prayer, BB, 63).

Meditation 7

Sin and Me

(After SE, #52)

For the past two weeks we have been considering two ancient models of sin: the sin of the angels and the sin of the first humans. This week we want to look at sin in our own lives.

People in 12 Step recovery do this early in their return to full humanity: they write down their "grosser handicaps" (BB, 71 – Step Four) and then share them with themselves, God, and another human being (Step Five). The point of this effort is to see what our part was in the disastrous relationships in which we have been involved. Most addicts have a lively sense of the harms others have done them, but are too ashamed to examine the harms they have done others. These Steps enable them to mature beyond shame and projection, and to take responsibility for what they have done, drinking or not.

This week we will probably want to see the harm we have done in the light of our meditations for the last two weeks. As in the cases of the angels and our first parents, it's a matter of self-will: "If [our] arrangements would only stay put, if only people would do as [we] wished, the show would be great" (BB, 60-61). "[W]e had to quit playing God" (BB, 62), which has been the chief temptation from the first for human beings.

As Bill points out in the searching analysis of human brokenness in chapter 5 of the Big Book, which I have been quoting liberally the last few weeks, a world full of

19

oversized and colliding egos is a miserable, hellish place. This is the real source of the alienation and the loneliness from which so many addicts suffer. We are so focused on what we think we must have to live that we have little sense of how our rapacity looks to other people. Nor is there an obvious way out. When I was newly sober and pondering these matters, I felt like I was being asked to give up my way just so some other persons could have theirs, and I naturally wondered what entitled them. The answer, of course, must lie in the will of a power bigger than me and my will, and bigger than you and yours. In our prayer this week, let us ask for "knowledge of God's will for us and the power to carry it out" (Step Eleven).

Second Prelude, to Go: Dear God, give me knowledge of your will; I already know too much about mine.

Meditation 8

Colloquy with Christ on the Cross

(SE, #53, 54)

For the last three weeks we have been pondering sin as committed by God's creatures, including ourselves. The point of stressing God as Creator (cf. the 7th Step Prayer) is that sin is our attempt to set aside the purpose for which we were created, to decide for ourselves what is to become of us.

Our prayer this week considers the climax to which Ignatius comes in the course of his threefold meditation on sin. What are we going to do, having fully acknowledged our powerlessness over all the attachments that impede our realization of God's hopes for us? Ignatius suggests we hold a "colloquy" with Christ, and specifically with Christ on the cross. He defines what he means by "colloquy" (from two Latin words) – "speaking exactly as one friend to another."

Note that this is a conversation between *friends*. Note, too, that the subject matter is not "What have I done *to* Christ?" Ignatius doesn't want us to retreat into shame and stay immobilized there. One of the standard pitfalls for addicts is to wallow in vast, unspecific shame, and to make this an excuse to keep using. We are not Christ's enemies, somehow tormenting him with our moral failings; we are Christ's friends, whom he hopes to change by what he undergoes. Just as with Step Two, this colloquy with Christ is meant to strike a spark of hope, not of despair.

And so Ignatius suggests that we ask ourselves, not "What have I done *to* Christ?" but rather "What have I done for Christ? What am I doing for Christ? What ought I to do for Christ?" In other words, the feelings our prayer should arouse are 12th Step feelings – gratitude and the desire to serve. Miserably obsessing on our failures is another form – although it may be the subtlest – of the "selfishness," the "self-centeredness" that is "the root of our troubles" (BB, 62). It's pretty narcissistic to think that Jesus' suffering is all about us; doesn't it make more sense to think that it's all about him, about his gratitude to his God, about his desire to serve all his human sisters and brothers? Trust me – loving service is where the Spiritual Exercises, like the 12 Steps, are going to take us. But don't take my word for it; why not check in with your guide about how your "searching and fearless" self-examination is going so far?

Second Prelude, to Go: Lord Jesus, what have I done for you? What am I doing for you? What ought I to do for you – today?

Meditation 9

Locked Up

(After SE, #47)

What is it like to be trapped in an addictive process? In our meditation this week, Ignatius offers some vivid imagery. As before, it might seem strained to anyone but an addict; addicts will probably perceive it as understated reportage.

Ignatius asks me to "see in imagination my soul as a prisoner in this corruptible body, and to consider my whole composite being as an exile here on earth, cast out to live among brute beasts. I said my whole composite being, body and soul." Rather than as a philosophical description of the human person, let's consider this as a poetic sketch of an "attached" woman or man.

As poetry it is thoroughly apt. Bill W. uses some of the same imagery to describe alcoholism: for instance, he speaks of "the alcoholic who has lost everything and is locked up" (BB, 62). "Exile" conjures up the terrible sense of isolation addicts feel, which Bill calls "the chilling vapor that is loneliness" (BB, 151). "Composite being" is a fair description of the sense of conflicting impulses that threatens to tear the addict apart; "corruptible" evokes the decay, the feeling of falling apart, even physically, that is often part of the addictive process, which almost always ages its victims prematurely. "Brute beasts" turn up in the similes we use to describe our drinking or using: "I drank like a fish" or "a pig," "I was a hog in my relationships," and so on. (Perhaps this is not even fair to the actual ani-

23

mals – Babe is much nicer than most addicts.) What this imagery really points out is that our addiction made us less than human – especially painful if we had started out trying to be angels, to be somehow more than human.

St. Paul sums this up in theological, not poetic, language: "I cannot even understand my own actions. I do not do what I want to do but what I hate. . . . What a wretched human being I am! Who can free me from this body under the power of death?" (Rom 7:15, 24). His answer – and ours – is to go back to the Christ of the Colloquy, the Higher Power of our Second Step: "All praise to God, through Jesus Christ our Lord!" In the light of the freedom from compulsion, from loneliness and death, that Christ has wrought for me, "what ought I to do for Christ?" (SE, #53).

Second Prelude, to Go: Lord Jesus, I thank you for calling me out of prison to freedom. What ought I to do in return?

Meditation 10

The Chained Man in the Cave

(Mk 5)

"[Jesus and his disciples] came to Gerasene [i.e., non-Jewish, Gentile] territory on the other side of the lake. As he got out of the boat, he was immediately met by a man from the tombs who had an unclean spirit. The man had taken refuge among the tombs; he could no longer be restrained even with a chain. In fact, he had frequently been secured with handcuffs and chains, but had pulled the chains apart and smashed the fetters. No one had proved strong enough to tame him. Uninterruptedly night and day, amid the tombs and on the hillsides, he screamed and gashed himself with stones. . . . 'What is your name?' Jesus asked him. 'Legion is my name,' he answered. 'There are hundreds of us.'" (Mk 5:1-5, 9)

St. Ignatius uses several images to convey the feeling of powerlessness that comes with a growing awareness of our attachments, of our sinfulness. In last week's meditation he spoke of a sense of being trapped, of being a prisoner. He returns to this image in a later meditation (see SE, #74), and there urges retreatants to consider themselves "prisoners," "loaded with chains," "bound with fetters." This way of describing sinfulness, of what it feels like to need salvation by a greater power, has deep roots in our Jewish tradition: Scholars tell us that in Biblical Hebrew, the root for the word salvation, *YS*, connotes being let out of prison, escaping from a tight spot (the name "Jesus," "Savior," comes from this root).

Addicts should have no trouble identifying with these feelings. The essence of addiction is an ever-narrowing range of increasingly miserable options; the essence of recovery is a sudden widening of possibility. Specifically, the addict who is writing this has always recognized a brother in the Gerasene man in Mark's Gospel, as I note in the last meditation of my next book (see Meditation for Thanksgiving, Year C). The details of his life may seem lurid, but they're actually not so far from where addiction takes us.

He knew profound alienation from other people, living in caves, non-kosher places because of the dead buried there. He knew what it was like to be trapped – "he had frequently been secured with handcuffs and chains." People had chained him, perhaps even with his compliance, in hopes that he would not act out, but he broke the chains – only to use this "freedom" to continue to destroy himself (he "gashed himself with stones"). This man was in the same utterly powerless place as an alcoholic whom Carl Jung unsuccessfully treated. Jung told his "utterly hopeless" patient that "he would have to place himself under lock and key or hire a bodyguard if he expected to live long" (BB, 26). Finally, "Legion" is a fair description of the "committee" that is constantly convening in some addicts' minds, sending out a stream of contradictory impulses and decisions.

This week let's continue to recall our own First Step. Let's return in memory to the times in our lives when we felt bound, trapped, hopeless in the face of an attachment. But let's recall as well the end of the story of the Gerasene man. After his encounter with Jesus, the people who had known him during his insanity "were seized with fear" to see "the man who had been possessed by Legion sitting fully clothed and perfectly sane" (Mk 5:15). For him, as for us, the First Step was followed by a Second, by a restoration to sanity by a power greater than himself. And eventually, having had his spiritual awakening, he will work a 12th Step: Jesus tells the man not to come with him, but to "[g]o home" – you *can* go home once you're restored to sanity – "and make it clear to [your family] how much the Lord in mercy has done for you" (Mk 5:19). We should keep returning to the questions of the colloquy: in the light of "how much the Lord in mercy has done for [me]," "What have I done for Christ? What am I doing for Christ? What ought I to do for Christ?"

Second Prelude, to Go: Lord Jesus, thank you for showing me great mercy. Show me how to use my freedom to serve you better.

Meditation 11

The Uses of My Past

During this First Week of the Exercises, Ignatius urges us to consider our past, not in a spirit of "worry, remorse or morbid reflection" (BB, 86), but in the light of chances for service we may up till now have been too attached to grasp ("What have I done for Christ?"). Some people would say that recovering addicts need not, or perhaps even should not, examine how they have fallen short of their ethical beliefs during their addiction, but such self-scrutiny is at the heart of the Twelve Step approach to recovery.

One of the A.A. Promises describes the attitude we should take toward our past: "We will not regret the past nor wish to shut the door on it" (BB, 83). This is more paradoxical than it may at first seem: surely if we addicts keep the door open to our pasts, we will have clear sight of plenty of things we should regret? Note, however, that the Promises kick in "before we are halfway through" the Ninth Step, the Step in which we go to people we have harmed and try to find a better way to relate to them. A clear view of the past is essential if we are going to behave differently now; we can't regret the clarity that leads to healed relationships.

But there is another reason why we "will not regret the past." From a Twelfth Step point of view, our past is alchemically transmuted into a treasure for other people. As Bill ruefully observes in "The Family Afterward": "The alcoholic's past thus becomes the principal asset of the family and frequently it is almost the only one!" (BB, 124). Another one of the Promises puts it this way: "No matter how far down the scale we have gone, we will see how our experience can benefit others" (BB, 84). This may even involve suffering on our part – for the sake of the newcomer, "we do recount and almost relive the horrors of our past" (BB, 132) – but this suffering is redemptive, as was the suffering of Christ on the cross. At the Easter Vigil on Holy Saturday, the most solemn night of the Christian year, an ancient hymn is chanted, which says in part "O happy fault [the "fall" of Adam and Eve] that merited so great a savior!" Similarly, some recovering people style themselves "grateful alcoholics" because the "fault" of their alcoholism has "merited so great" an experience of liberation, good for them and for others. Once again during this First Week, we end with the colloquy with Jesus, whose "experience" on the cross has so greatly "benefited" us that we will want to do things for Christ in return.

Second Prelude, to Go: Lord Jesus, show me how I can use my past pain to bring healing, so that I may more closely follow you.

Application of the Senses

(See SE, #66-70)

In the course of the Exercises, Ignatius suggests many different forms of prayer – and of course there are others that may work for you that he didn't even think of; a good director can suggest some. This week I invite you to try one that some people find helpful, particularly sensate people (I'm more of a verbal person myself – rather obviously). The point is to use whatever works for you – mind, imagination, memory, or (this week) your senses.

The concept here is straightforward. Ignatius invites us to put ourselves in a particular scene, and then see it, hear what the people in the scene say, touch people or objects, even smell and taste things, as a way to get ideas from our heads to our hearts and guts. Ignatius often uses this method in the many meditations on the life of Jesus that will occupy the remaining three weeks of the Exercises. But he introduces this technique during the First Week, when what we are praying over is more conceptual. This method is that much more useful in making vivid what might otherwise be hazy or colorless.

So what does the First Step smell like? How does powerlessness taste? What are the sounds of unmanageability? If sin were an object we could handle, what would it feel like? What does attachment look like?

The Big Book is full of suggestive passages – Bill W. had a weakness for just the kind of purple prose that can appeal to the senses. In your prayer this week, you might want to use your senses to appreciate more deeply a familiar passage like this one, from "A Vision for You" (Chapter 11 of the Big Book): "The less people tolerated us, the more we withdrew from society, from life itself." So far this is true enough – addiction isolates of its nature – but fairly abstract. But now Bill ratchets up his rhetoric: "As we became subjects of King Alcohol, shivering denizens of his mad realm, the chilling vapor that is loneliness settled down." What does the "mad" (i.e., "insane") kingdom of alcohol, of drug addiction, look like? Stunted trees? A desert full of mirages? Haunted houses or castles? What sounds does one hear in this kingdom? Sobs? Cackles of contemptuous laughter? Empty promises? What does it smell or taste like – a half-empty beer can full of cigarette butts? Finally, what does loneliness feel like? Bill describes it as a clammy fog settling on our skin, like a cold night sweat.

He goes on: The chilling vapor "thickened, ever becoming blacker" (it goes from gray fog to a black cloud all around us). "Some of us sought out sordid places, hoping to find understanding companionship and approval." Stop again: what were the sights and sounds and smells of the places our addiction took us to? Even if we were home drinkers, the rooms where we did our drinking had their own sounds and sights. I can recall the T.V. room in a Jesuit residence: I am sitting blearily in the dark, next to an overflowing ashtray, watching the opening montage from a "Love Boat" rerun, tearfully singing along with the theme.

Finally, Bill winds up with an allusion to one of the grimmest books of the Bible, the Book of Revelations: "Momentarily we did [find companionship] – then would come oblivion and the awful awakening to face the hideous Four Horsemen – Terror, Bewilderment, Frustration,

Despair. Unhappy drinkers who read this page will understand!" (BB, 151). We will understand, with more than just a mental understanding; we can picture these terrible riders. How does Terror sound? What does Despair look like? Does Frustration taste bitter? If we could touch Bewilderment, would it feel cold and rotting?

They say in A.A. that if you've forgotten your last drink, you're in danger of taking another. In our prayer this week, let's remember, with all our senses, the past, so that, to paraphrase Santayana, we need not be condemned to repeat it. And let's continue to talk as a friend to Jesus on the cross, because God "rescued us from the power of darkness and brought us into the kingdom of God's beloved Son" (Col 1:13).

Second Prelude, to Go: Lord Jesus, help me to leave bitterness behind so I may better taste sweet freedom.

Meditation 13

To Hell and Back

In one of his meditations (SE, #65) Ignatius suggests that the retreatant contemplate hell. In fact, he suggests that we use the prayer method of the Application of the Senses, which I described last week.

As I mentioned in Meditation Five, a lot of addicts feel like they have been to hell and back in the course of their addiction and recovery. The Big Book describes the "spiritual awakening" of one early A.A. member very much in these terms. Like a lot of alcoholics, this man felt he had been subjected to "an overdose of religious education" as a child. Like many alcoholics, as an adult he "rebelled" against all this forced piety, but found that, by his own power, he could only respond to life's disasters with an "overdose" of alcohol, which brought him, like the Gerasene man, "to the point of self-destruction." He was 12th-Stepped by "an alcoholic who had known a spiritual experience," but he believed that this kind of experience was impossible for him. At this moment, squarely in the middle of a First Step, with no notion how to get on to any other Steps, "he felt as though he lived in hell" (BB, 56).

This is pretty much the "hell" that most addicts have known. The essence of hell, as Sartre's play *No Exit* suggests, is to be locked into a tangle of unsatisfied needs, with no hope at all that it will ever be any different. This is the daily fare of the addicted person. Ignatius advises us to pay a visit this week to this place where we used to live, the better to appreciate "what we used to be like, what happened, and what we are like now" (BB, 58).

The man who "felt as though he lived in hell" goes on with his story: he "recounts that," after thinking to himself, *"Who are you to say there is no God?"* [italics in original], he "was overwhelmed by a conviction of the Presence of God. It poured over and through him with the certainty and majesty of a great tide at flood. The barriers he had built through the years were swept away. He stood in the Presence of Infinite Power and Love. He had stepped from bridge to shore. . . ." (BB, 56).

Like this member of A.A., we have subsequently had "deep and effective spiritual experiences" (BB, 25). Although our "revelation" may not have been as "sudden" as his, we believe, like him, and like the Gerasene man, that "God has restored us all to our right minds" (BB, 57). In the light of this, "what ought I to do for Christ," for "Infinite Power and Love" (BB, 56)?

Second Prelude, to Go: Lord Jesus, what can I do for you who have brought me out of prison into light and fresh air?

Note: Move on or Pause?

A fundamental principle in making the Spiritual Exercises is that you linger over meditations, or over Weeks, where you are getting what you need, but that eventually you will sense that it's time to move on. This is one reason why it helps to be making the Exercises with a Director, who can "discern" (an important Ignatian term – see Meditation 51, below) with you exactly where you are on your journey. If you do have a guide, you might ask her or him at this point whether you should go deeper or go farther. But however you are using this book, do not feel like you have to spend only one week on a given meditation, or do every single meditation I offer. Move on to the next meditation when you're ready; move on to the next Week when you're ready, no matter which meditation you're on.

Meditation 14

Taking Stock

(After SE, #56)

A sober Jesuit friend of mine once waggishly observed that the A.A. 5th Step, in which we share written self-inventories with a trustworthy listener, was a lot like the Catholic practice of a General Confession, "except that in the 5th Step you tell the truth." Since the 5th Step is such a crucial Step on the 12 Step path – the Big Book, unusually stern on this point, says that "[i]f we skip this vital step, we may not overcome drinking" – most 12 Steppers will not be put off by Ignatius' suggestion that those walking the path of his Exercises make "a record of [their] sins."

Ignatius and Bill W. are both eminently practical about this. Ignatius speaks of a "record"; the word, *proceso* in the original Spanish, means "trial transcript." Bill, a failed stockbroker, was fond of mercantile imagery, and so calls the list of "shortcomings" that the recovering person draws up an "inventory." In either version, the point is that it all gets written down in black and white.

Why? Bill aptly describes the mental state of newly sober persons: "Coming to [their] senses, [they are] revolted at certain episodes [they] vaguely remember[ ]" (BB, 73). As long as things stay morally vague, recovering persons are not going to be able to attain what we now call "values clarification." For ethical and psychological development to resume, recovering persons have to grasp clearly, and assume responsibility for, what they have done

– *all* they have done, but no more than what they have done.

To further assist this sorting-out process, Bill and Ignatius suggest certain broad categories that people should consider in writing up their lapses. Bill suggests three large areas: resentments, fears, and sexual (and perhaps other) relationships. This makes sense: most of the harm we do as human beings we do in our relationships with others; and most of that harm stems from those two most basic drives, anger (we've lost something) or fear (we might not get, or might lose, something). If we are going to live contented lives, we will have to conduct our relationships in a new, less angry and fearful way.

Ignatius for his part urges us to make a "searching" moral "process" by going over our lives in detail: we should remember "the place where I lived," "my dealings with others" (relationships), "the office I have held" i.e., my job (another arena where anger and fear and attachment can wreak havoc). Ignatius also suggests using the Seven Deadly Sins as a guide to self-examination (see SE, #244). Curiously, when Bill commented on the 4th Step in 1953, after having the Jesuit Father Eddie Dowling as a spiritual guide for thirteen years, he made the same suggestion.

But whatever the method of self-examination used, the point of this exercise is, again, not to become paralyzed with shame. Rather, let us ask for the grace this week to know our failings more clearly so we can ask God to remove them and thus help us to serve others better (cf. Steps Six and Seven). This growth in freedom is the purpose of the Exercises and of the Twelve Steps.

As we did last week, let's continue to ask what we can do for Christ, who has restored us to sanity.

Second Prelude, to Go: "Dear God, I pray that you now remove from me every single defect of character which stands in the way of my usefulness to you and my fellows" (from the Seventh Step Prayer, BB, 76).

Meditation 15

Coming to Order

I mentioned before that Ignatius, like Gerald May, talks about "attachments" as a besetting spiritual problem for human beings. Ignatius calls them "inordinate attachments." For this week's meditation, let's consider a variation on this: Ignatius tells us to ask God for the "favor" of "understanding . . . the disorder of my actions, that . . . I may amend my life and put it in order" (SE, #63). In other words, sin happens when our desires, or what Bill W. calls our "instincts," get out of order, or "far exceed their proper function" (12 X 12, 42). And disorder, excess, are second nature to addicts: "For thousands of years we have been demanding more than our share of security, prestige, and romance. . . . Never was there enough of what we thought we wanted" (12 X 12, 71). Before public drunkenness was decriminalized, alcoholics were routinely arrested for "disorderly conduct"; how right the law was, in a spiritual sense.

It makes sense, then, that recovery can be perceived as a restoration of order. Indeed, some A.A.'s who are uncomfortable with the word "God" have turned it into an acronym: G.O.D. as they understand God is "Good Orderly Direction." If you have been going in circles or riding off in all directions at once for years, orderly progress in just one direction can feel like a touch of the divine.

Last week's meditation asked us to recall our past Fourth Steps, or perhaps to write an updated one in the light of what our retreat experience so far may have uncovered. Taking another Fifth Step about now might be a good idea, because Twelve Steppers get a deeper knowledge of just how they get broken, get out of order, by studying the Fourth Column on their Fourth Steps ("what is my part in this disordered relationship?"), and by going over the "record" of their lives with a trusted advisor. Knowledge of disorder is pretty much what the Big Book refers to as "causes and conditions" (64), or as "big chunks of truth" about ourselves (71).

In our meditation this week, let's abide in the spirit of Steps 6 and 7: as we acquire a deeper sense of our disordered attachments, we will become more "ready to have God remove" them, and grow in "that basic ingredient of all humility, a desire to seek and do God's will" (12 X 12, 72).

Secondlude, to Go: "My Creator, I am now willing that you should have all of me, good and bad" (from the 7th Step prayer – BB, 76).

Meditation 16

Amends

During this First Week of the Exercises, we have been paralleling the Steps. The meditations on sin correspond to the First Step; the Colloquy with Jesus on the Cross, to which we keep returning, is a kind of Second Step; and over the last couple of weeks we have looked at variations of Steps Four and Five and Steps Six and Seven. This week we will consider the process of making amends, which is taken up in Steps Eight and Nine.

Ignatius, like Bill W., ties the process of amends to a knowledge of the "disorder" of our lives. The Big Book puts it this way: "Let's look at *Steps Eight and Nine.* We have a list of all persons we have harmed and to whom we are willing to make amends. We made it when we took inventory. We subjected ourselves to a drastic self-appraisal. Now we go out to our fellows and repair the damage done in the past" (BB, 76; italics in original). Ignatius, in a passage I quoted last week, suggests a similar process: we are to ask God for several "favors," including "[a]n understanding of the disorder of my actions, that . . . I may amend my life and put it in order" (SE, #63).

The original Spanish for "amend" (*enmiende*) is worth studying: it carries several meanings, all relevant to Steps Eight and Nine. It can mean "to correct": when something is wrong, like the way we treat other people, we change it for the better. It can also mean "to compensate": if people have incurred losses, financial or emotional, because of our behavior to them, we try to make restitution to them.

Finally, it can mean to reform oneself, to become a different person; this is related to the first meaning, but stresses that the changed outward behavior flows from a changed heart, a changed view of life and of people and of God.

Interestingly, one thing that *enmiende* does *not* mean is "apologize." Bill W. would agree that "amends" goes much farther and deeper than mere apology: "A remorseful mumbling that we are sorry won't fill the bill at all" (BB, 83). For the long process of amendment to work, we will have to lean heavily on God, since what is required is an ongoing change of heart, from which will flow greater "order" in my relationships with others.

This would be a good week to say the Seventh Step Prayer often, especially the middle sentence: "I pray that you [Higher Power] now remove from me every single defect of character which stands in the way of my usefulness to you and my fellows" (BB, 76). If we are going to do great things for Christ, give great service, we will have to change and be changed.

"Amendment" is crucial in ending the loneliness that so powerfully gnaws at addicts. Bill W. says of Step Eight that "[i]t is the beginning of the end of isolation from our fellows and from God" (12 X 12, 82). And this is no doubt why the Promises are said to be "fulfilled among us" at "this phase of our development" (BB, 84, 83). In terms of the Exercises, if we have reached a point where we are now "willing" to make amends, in all the senses noted above, we are almost ready to leave the First Week – after some suggestions about bringing into our daily lives the principles and practices we have so far learned (see next meditation).

Second Prelude, to Go: "My Creator . . . I pray that you now remove from me every single defect of character

which stands in the way of my usefulness to you and my
fellows" (from the 7th Step Prayer – BB, 76).

Meditation 17

The Examen

Ignatius and Bill W. strongly support the "healthy practice" of regular self-examination; Bill, always the ex-stock-
broker, declares that it is "interesting and profitable" (12
X 12, 89). Bill, of course, likes the term "inventory"; Ignatius calls it the Examen. The Tenth Step of A.A. suggests
that the principles of stock-taking, humility, and amendment learned in working Steps Four through Nine be
practiced every day; Ignatius believes that the continued
practice of the Examen can keep the spirit of the Exercises alive in a retreatant.

Ignatius's "Method of Making the General Examina-
tion [Examen] of Conscience" (SE, #43) is fairly similar to
Bill's suggestions for doing a nightly 10th Step (BB, 86).
Ignatius, who is as fond of orderly steps as Bill, provides
five points for this examen.

"The first point is to give thanks to God our Lord for
the favors received." We are to begin our prayer, not with
our failings, but with a gratitude list for all God has done
for us and through us on this day. Bill didn't think of including a gratitude list at the time he wrote the Big Book;
but when he wrote his commentary on the Steps a decade
later, he fine-tuned Step Ten. (Perhaps he stumbled
across this idea while struggling with the deep depression
that plagued him during the 1940s.) In the 12 X 12, he
suggests, "This is a good place to remember that inven-
tory-taking is not always done in red ink. It's a poor day
indeed when we haven't done *something* right. . . . Good

44

intentions, good thoughts, and good acts are there for us to see" (93 – Bill's italics). He also suggests that a nightly inventory should conclude thus: "Having so considered our day, not omitting to take due note of things well done . . . we can truly thank God for the blessings we have received and sleep in good conscience" (12 X 12, 95).

Ignatius's second point is "to ask for grace to know my sins and to rid myself of them." Note that this is not self-laceration; we are asking for "grace," a "favor," a "present," from God. Bill makes a similar point by saying "we *constructively* review our day" (emphasis added). In his third point, Ignatius bids us to "go over" our day, "one hour after another," considering "thoughts," "words," and "deeds." Bill is a little more specific: we are to search out resentments, selfishness, dishonesty, and fear, some of the most common moral lapses among addicts; we are to take note of any amends we owe, or anything "kept . . . to ourselves which should be discussed with another person at once." Then, says Bill, we are to consider the occasions during the day when we were "kind and loving." The desired result of all this, for Ignatius as for Bill, is greater service of God and our neighbor; we are seeking greater freedom from all those attachments that "diminish our usefulness to others" (BB, 86).

Ignatius's last two points are almost identical with the sentence with which Bill ends his description of the daily Tenth Step. Ignatius puts it like this: "The fourth point will be to ask pardon of God our Lord for my faults. . . . The fifth point will be to resolve to amend [*enmienda* again] with the grace of God." Bill's words: "After making our review we ask God's forgiveness and inquire what corrective measures should be taken."

Both Bill and Ignatius also offer suggestions about other forms of inventory: "On awakening let us think about the twenty-four hours ahead" (Bill, BB, 86); "First, in the morning, immediately on rising, one should resolve to guard carefully against the particular . . . defect" that is especially troublesome to a person (Ignatius, SE, #24). Bill is also a fan of the "spot-check inventory" (12 X 12, 89 and ff.), taken "[a]s we go through the day . . . when agitated or doubtful" (BB, 87); Ignatius in his turn urges retreatants to inculcate awareness of their moral progress, or lack of it, from time to time during the course of the day.

For neither Bill nor Ignatius are these practices meant to be "joy-killers as well as time-consumers" (12 X 12, 89). They are instead methods to continue our ethical and spiritual "development" (BB, 83), interrupted by our addiction, resumed with our recovery, and "under the grace of God" (12 X 12, 125) maintained for the rest of our lives.

Second Prelude, to Go: Dear God, forgive my faults and show me how, with your grace, to amend my life.

✚

Second Week

Before we begin the Second Week, I want to reflect on the point we have reached in our study of the two paths, of Bill W. and of Ignatius. During most of the First Week, we were traveling with Ignatius down a path that paralleled many of the Steps, as I mentioned a few weeks ago. In fact, I have already cited all but three of the Steps, and you may be wondering what is left to consider for the rest of the retreat. Or you may be wondering what happened to the missing three Steps: Three, Eleven, and Twelve.

Another peculiarity about this "retreat" up to this point has been its emphasis on the retreatant rather than upon God. Only in the often-repeated Colloquy with Christ on the cross has Ignatius specified who our Higher Power is: Christ is the source of the healing we need to overcome our attachments. So far, then, our retreat has been largely a Second Step experience of God: we have recalled our powerlessness, the cry for help we uttered from the depth of our First Step, and the sudden (or gradual) sense of liberation that came our way, a liberation that Christians associate with Christ and his redemptive suffering. At that point we may have taken a kind of Third Step: we trusted Christ enough that we continued with the painful self-scrutiny embodied in Steps Four through Nine, as well as in the First Week.

Where are we now, then? As we begin the Second Week, I think we are called to take another, more searching Third Step. Perhaps we will want to take it formally, with our spiritual guides, as we begin this next phase. In the Third Step we took earlier, the emphasis was on us, on our turning over our lives and wills; this time the emphasis will be on God as we understand God, the One to whom we turn over our lives and wills.

To put this another way, the remainder of the retreat will be Eleventh Step work. In our Colloquy with Christ on the Cross, we made a "conscious contact with God"; but we may not know very much about this God, this Jesus the Christ. Or we may be struggling with a distorted view of him, just as many newly sober people struggle with a misshapen picture of a monstrous God, left over from their distant childhoods. So our goal for the rest of the retreat is to "improve our conscious contact" with Christ; and the best way to do that is to study his life, death, and resurrection. Ignatius repeatedly tells us to ask for this grace during the Second Week: "an intimate knowledge of our Lord [Jesus], who has become a human being for me, that I may love Him more and follow Him more closely" (SE, #104).

As we shall see in the course of the Second Week, to know Jesus is to realize that his personal identity is completely intertwined with doing the will of God, whom he called "Abba," an affectionate term for "Father." As we study Jesus' life, we will simultaneously be pondering how we should best live our lives. In other words, as we "improve our conscious contact with God" – the God whom Jesus preached – we will also concurrently be "praying only for knowledge of [God's] will for us and the power to carry that out" (BB, 59). The rest of the retreat will lead us to our concluding Contemplation, when we will in a fuller way "get" the love of God; and at that point, as the retreat ends, we will be ready to put that love into action in our lives. We will be readier – less attached, more free – to work our Twelfth Step.

The Kingdom of Christ (Part I)

Ignatius does not ask us to begin our study of the life of Christ with His birth. Instead, he begins with a more global meditation, as a transition between the First and the Second Week. Before we take a look at Jesus' life, Ignatius suggests that we ask "Who is this Jesus? What is he about?" This can be particularly important for people who have learned to think of Christ as icily perfect and vindictive, someone who found the human struggles in which he chose to immerse himself to be absurdly easy to surmount, and who therefore has little sympathy with those of us who find life very difficult.

When Ignatius asked himself, "Who is Jesus for me?," he naturally was attracted to the image of Jesus as King. Ignatius was a soldier and a courtier before his conversion, and so had spent nearly half his life trying to give good service to earthly kings. A world with royalty made sense to him. Nevertheless, in this meditation he offers a vision of kingship which is a bit different from the kind of royalty he had known. And Ignatius's Christ the King is also far from the chilly, prissy Jesus I sketched above.

But the kingdom is not just a pet concept of Ignatius'; it is also closely linked to Jesus' sense of himself and of his mission, as set out in the New Testament. In Mark's Gospel, the first written, there is no account of Jesus' birth or childhood. Instead, after a few verses on John the Baptist, who warms up the crowd for Jesus, and a few verses more on Christ's preparation for his ministry,

Christ appears, at verse 15, and the first words out of his mouth are "This is the time of fulfillment. The reign of God is at hand! Reform your lives and believe in the gospel!" The kingdom, or "reign," of God was an essential theme in the message of Jesus and his followers: the word appears 162 times in the New Testament (the word for "judgment," incidentally, only appears 48 times).

"Kingdom" in the New Testament is a very rich concept; but for our purposes, let's go back to what it meant specifically to Ignatius. Given his experience, he naturally moved from the Kingdom Jesus announced to Jesus as King – a move that Jesus himself rarely makes in the Gospels. Ignatius thought of King Jesus as being similar to an earthly king, a greatly idealized one, something like the British King Arthur, or a king in one of the medieval romances of which Ignatius had been so fond as a younger man. He asks the retreatant to imagine such a human king, and puts these words in the king's mouth: " . . . whoever wishes to join with me in this enterprise must be content with the same food, drink, clothing, etc. as mine. So, too, they must work with me by day, and watch with me by night, etc., that as they have had a share in toil with me, afterwards they may share in the victory with me" (SE, #93).

Ignatius emphasizes two things: the very down-to-earth struggles that will be required to bring about the Kingdom ("this enterprise"), and the fact that this king, despite his royal birth, is willing to share the gritty realities of the campaign – indeed, he seems to undergo them first, and invites us to follow his lead. Already, this analogy of an earthly king is preparing us to see Christ the King in a different way: not as a rigid, self-righteous being high above the messiness of life, but as someone deeply, painfully involved in it.

When Ignatius goes on to round out the analogy of the earthly king by giving the Call of Christ the King, he underscores this point. Christ says, "[W]hoever wishes to join me in this enterprise must be willing to labor with me, that by following me in suffering, they may follow me in glory" (SE, #95). Jesus calls us to work and suffering, but he gets his hands dirty first.

During this week, let's ask to know Jesus better, to know the *real* Jesus. And as we get to know this Jesus, as he grows on us, let's frequently recall the conclusions Ignatius draws from these reflections: "Consider what the answer of good subjects ought to be to a king so generous and noble-minded" (SE, #94); and "Those who wish to give greater proof of their love . . . will . . . offer themselves entirely for the work" (SE, #97). We are preparing for another, richer Third Step (see next week). We are being invited to say more whole-heartedly to God, "God, I offer myself to Thee – to build with me and to do with me as Thou wilt."

Second Prelude, to Go: "God, I offer myself to Thee – to build with me and to do with me as Thou wilt" (from the Third Step Prayer – BB, 63).

The Kingdom of Christ (Part II)

I would like to pick up where we left off last week: let's continue reflecting on the Kingdom of Christ. For some older Jesuits, this is one of the peak moments of the Exercises; but for Jesuits of my generation, who came of age in the egalitarian 1960s, the idea of kingship is pretty blank (Watergate didn't help, either, come to think of it).

The concept of royalty can, I think, be viewed as a metaphor that meant a lot to a Renaissance man like Ignatius of Loyola, but which may not mean much to someone these days. But what then is the meaning behind the metaphor? As a matter of fact, one could argue that Jesus transformed – "deconstructed," as the post-moderns say – the meaning of the word "kingdom." He spent his entire ministry talking about, and enacting, this new understanding of "kingdom" as a community of mutual service. Much of his struggle with his contemporaries was about their stubborn refusal to accept his redefinition of "kingdom."

On the night before he died, he made a last effort to get the point across to his closest friends, who were nearly as baffled by his radical transvaluation of "kingdom" as were the rest of Jesus' hearers. In the Gospel of Luke, who is especially good on Jesus' unique understanding of "kingdom," Jesus says this as part of his farewell address to his disciples at the Last Supper: "Earthly kings lord it over their people. Those who exercise authority over them are called their benefactors. Yet it cannot be that way with you. Let the greater among you be as the junior, the leader as the servant" (Lk 22:25-26; as we shall see in the Third Week, even after this they didn't grasp his point).

This new notion of kingship as service was hinted at in last week's meditation: Ignatius stresses the willingness of his *earthly* king to undergo earthly hardship in the midst of his subjects. This week I want to bring this to the forefront: to say that we are subjects of *Christ* the King is another way of saying that we are disciples of Jesus, who came, "not to be served by others, but to serve" (Mt 20:28).

This aspect of Christ shows up in the Preludes that Ignatius offers to the meditation on the Kingdom of Christ. In contrast to the imagery of conquest he employs in the body of the meditation, here he speaks more directly of following Jesus in ministry: "First Prelude. Here it will be to see in imagination the synagogues, villages, and towns where Christ our Lord preached. Second Prelude. I will ask for the grace I desire. Here it will be to ask of our Lord the grace not to be deaf to His call, but prompt and diligent to accomplish His most holy will" (SE, #91). The "enterprise" of Jesus is carried out by itinerant preaching, not by battles fought on foaming chargers.

So . . . do we want a piece of this "enterprise," this paradoxical kind of kingdom? If we do, perhaps it's time to take another Third Step. From early in my recovery I have thought of Step Three as the discipleship step. In Step One we cry out for help, like Peter drowning in the Sea of Galilee; in Step Two, a power greater than ourselves shows up, pulls us up from the abyss, and calms the storm (see Meditation 34, below). Step Three seems to me to follow Two with rigorous logic: if you have found a Power that can help you with the biggest problem you've got, it's only good sense to turn over everything else you have and are to that Power. Or, as the New Testament puts it, if you have found the One you have been looking for all your life, leave everything behind and follow him. During this week, continue to go over the words of the Third Step Prayer, especially the last two sentences.

Second Prelude, to Go: "Take away my difficulties, that victory over them may bear witness to those I would help of Thy Power, Thy Love, and Thy Way of Life. May I do Thy will always!" (from the Third Step Prayer – BB, 63).

Meditation 20

The Incarnation

(SE, #102 ff.)

Last week I mentioned that an older generation of Jesuits seemed to find in the meditation on the Kingdom of Christ their personal core of the Exercises. For me, and for some Jesuits of my generation, this meditation on the Incarnation of Jesus is the focal point of spiritual energies. The Incarnation – the theological idea that in Jesus God put on humanity – takes on a very 12th Step spin in Ignatius's vision. He wants us to reflect, not upon the "how" of this mystery, but upon the "why," and the "why" is a matter of carrying a message to people who badly need it. The Son of God becomes human to save humans.

Ignatius takes us through three points, employing respectively sight, hearing, and mind. The meditation first offers an extraordinarily sweeping vista. It invites us to consider the world from the point of view of the Trinity: "First Point. This will be to see the different persons [human *and* divine]. First, those on the face of the earth, in such great diversity of dress and in manner of acting. Some are white, some black; some at peace, and some at war; some weeping, some laughing; some well, some sick; some coming into the world, and some dying, etc." (SE, #106).

This is a very "catholic" vision, in the original sense of "all-embracing." Already there's a hint at service in the references to those "at war," the "weeping," the "sick," the "dying." There's a similar passage near the end of the First Part (the theoretical part, pages 1-164 in the 3rd edi-

56

tion, before the Stories) of the Big Book: "Near you, alcoholics are dying helplessly like people in a sinking ship. If you live in a large place, there are hundreds. High and low, rich and poor, these are future fellows of Alcoholics Anonymous" (BB, 152). If we share these visions of an urgently needy world, we will want to do something, to "carry" some kind of healing "message" to those "dying helplessly." During this Second Week, we are being called to know Jesus more. To know him is to grasp his message; and to carry that message is to become a disciple, to work a 12th Step.

Ignatius continues with another sense, hearing: "Second Point. This will be to listen to what the persons on the face of the earth say, that is, how they speak to one another, swear and blaspheme, etc." (SE, #107). There is a sense here of a great chorus of human sounds, including dark sounds – but in that "etc." there are also lullabies and the endearments of lovers, laughter and the conversation of old friends. Ignatius stresses the sounds of misery, though, because these are the sounds made by those who are "dying helplessly like people in a sinking ship."

Finally, Ignatius gives the divine context for, and the divine response to, what we have seen and heard. The Trinity has seen and heard all that the retreatant has seen and heard: "Third Point. This will be to consider what the persons on the face of the earth do, for example, wound, kill, and go down to hell. Also what the Divine Persons do, namely, work the most holy Incarnation, etc. Likewise, what the Angel [Gabriel, the angel of the Annunciation; see Lk 1:26-38] and our Lady [Mary, the mother of Jesus] do; how the Angel carries out the office of ambassador; and how our Lady humbles herself, and offers thanks to the Divine Majesty" (SE, #108).

Once again, Ignatius stresses the darkest things we humans are driven to do by our "natural desires . . . out of joint" (12 X 12, 42) – we "wound, kill, and go down to hell." This is the heart of the problem; this is our bottom as a species, that hunger and loss, and our nagging sense that there will never be enough of anything that matters to us, drive us to beat the life out of one another, as has happened from the First Family in the Book of Genesis on down.

God's response is not to turn aside in disgust and disapproval. Marvelously, "the Divine Persons" respond by "work[ing] the most holy Incarnation," by diving into the murderous wreck. And of course we know that Jesus, the Word made flesh, will eventually be murdered as well; this much was already forecast in the Colloquy of the First Week. By contrast to ordinary human (and angelic) willfulness, the Angel and Mary act out the proper response of creatures to their Creator: they "carr[y] out" God's will, and behave with humility and gratitude.

This meditation also contains a colloquy, to which we will often want to return this week, and in the weeks that will follow. Ignatius tells us to end our prayer like this: "Colloquy . . . I will beg for grace to follow and imitate more closely our Lord, who has just become human for me." For me – and for all of us.

This week you might want to keep in mind Joan Osbourne's song, "One of Us": "What if God was one of us/ Just a slob, like one of us?" This is pretty much the point of the Incarnation. Or you might want to identify with Jesus as a stranger coming to this strange planet on a Twelfth Step call, "jittery and alone." You'd be jittery too if you were trying to carry the message to such a violent species. But like that "jittery" rookie Twelfth-Stepper in the Big Book, Jesus is not really alone, because as Son of Abba he has "just now tapped into a source of power greater than [him]self" (BB, 163). The Letter to the Hebrews puts these words into Jesus' mouth at the moment of the Incarnation: "[A] body you [God] have prepared for me; . . . I have come to do your will, O God" (Heb 10:5, 7, quoting Ps 40).

Second Prelude, to Go: Lord Jesus, grant me the grace to follow and imitate you more closely, you who have just become human for me.

Note: On Using the Bible

For the next fourteen meditations, as well as for much of the Third and Fourth Weeks, we will be following Ignatius' lead by using passages from the Gospels in our study of the life and death of Jesus. The Scripture passage for each Meditation will be listed at the beginning of it: please use a Bible to read that passage before you read the meditation, and then reread that passage, and perhaps its parallels in the other Gospels, in the course of each week. I have chosen favorite passages of mine; Ignatius lists others as well. And you may feel free to add, or substitute, parts of the Gospels that have meant a lot to you. If you have a retreat guide, she or he may also suggest certain passages that seem apt for where you are.

Meditation 21

Jesus Is Born

(Lk 2:1-20)

Having become human last week, the first order of business for Jesus is to get born. To be born human is to be born utterly helpless, utterly vulnerable, needing all the help you can get. Jesus is born into a middling situation: he has two loving parents to make sure he is clothed and sheltered, but he is born away from home, like many children of refugees. His parents are loving, but they are also poor, and powerless in the face of government authority ordering them to leave home for some kind of mindless bureaucratic purpose.

And yet this is somehow a royal child, too: Joseph is "of the lineage of David," and the bureaucratic mess ironically insures that Jesus the "Messiah" (the word means "anointed with oil," as kings were at their coronation) will be born "in royal David's city," Bethlehem (Lk 2:4, 11). And this child is more than royal – angels announce his birth.

So we are reminded of the Kingdom Meditation. Jesus *is* a king, but in a whole new sense of the term; for what kind of king would be satisfied with an entourage made up of shepherds, who clearly sleep out in the open with their flocks? The answer: a new kind of king, who will rule over a new kind of kingdom. Kings up to the time of Jesus, and particularly the great king of Israel, David, had struggled, often unsuccessfully, with rage and lust and violence: David was very much "a battleground for the instincts" (12 X 12, 44). But as the "multitude of the heavenly host" proclaims, Jesus the Messiah and Lord will rule over a peaceful kingdom.

During the course of this week, let us remember to be grateful for this message: beyond resentment and fear lie serenity and peace, because the birth of Jesus is "tidings [from the Greek word associated with our word "Gospel"] of great joy to be shared by the whole people" (Lk 2:10). The whole people, notice: even shepherds, even the poor, even drunks.

Second Prelude, to Go: "Glory to God in the highest, and peace on earth to everyone, since we have all been given the love of God."

Meditation 22

The Wise Men, Herod, and the Flight into Egypt

(Mt 2:1-18)

Once again this week, the question of the Kingdom arises, even though Jesus is still a baby, years away from the beginning of his preaching of that Kingdom. In this week's reading, a real earthly king appears, Herod. Even given that kings are often violent and oversexed, Herod was one of the worst ever, a real monster along the lines of Stalin and Hitler. This becomes clear at the end of the reading from Matthew, when his paranoia drives him to have children killed.

He is afraid that a rival king has been born, for so he has been assured by the "astrologers" (these are the "Three Wise Men," or the "Three Kings," of later Christmas legend). At the time of Jesus, many kings would have included among their advisors people who studied the stars to discern the king's fate; and Jewish kings, David, for example, had prophets as staff members. So Herod would be as used to putting credence in the word of astrologers as a modern chief of state would in reports from intelligence operatives (perhaps ill-advisedly in either case).

No wonder, then, that Herod, and the rest of the power elite – "the chief priests and scribes" – were "greatly disturbed" (Mt 2:3, 4). For all of them, the idea that a rival king has been born can only portend violence. Herod no doubt justified his massacre on the grounds that it would prevent greater violence down the road, when the "newborn king" was old enough to raise an army.

No one, at this point or later in Jesus' life, grasps the new kind of kingdom that Jesus is bringing, a kingdom that belongs to the "poor in spirit" (Mt 5:3). Or just maybe the "astrologers," who actually saw the child, caught onto this truth. In any event, we who have heard the whole story must surely notice what kind of "king" Jesus is: Jesus and his parents are so powerless that they become refugees, and have to escape to Egypt. Think of all the people throughout history who have barely gotten out with their lives before those in power swept through, killing all who weren't lucky enough to escape. Jesus is one of them.

There is irony here, of course – Jesus' conception of "kingdom" is so different from ours that it always leads to irony. The irony in this case is not just that running for your life is far from our usual notion of royal behavior. The upshot of this flight is also ironic: Herod's rage forces Jesus to spend time in Egypt; when he returns to the land of Israel, he will retrace the ancient journey of liberation of his people, led by Moses through the desert. His powerlessness and his flight in the end only prove that he is in fact the son of "a loving God" (Tradition Two), who calls him "out of Egypt" (Mt 2:15) to show us the way to "a new freedom" (BB, 83).

Meanwhile, Jesus' experience of exile only makes him that much more "one of us": the Joan Osbourne song goes on to talk about God, who is "one of us," "trying to find his way home." Jesus spent his life, from infancy on, trying to go home; he was especially thinking about his "home" on the night before his death (see John 13 and 14; the Greek word *menein*, "make a home with," is a favorite of John's in these chapters and elsewhere). So Jesus the exile is "one" with addicted people, who are "tortured" by "that terrible sense of isolation we've always had," and who come to know God above all in the "tremendously exciting" "sense of belonging" they get when they encounter groups of recovering people (12 X 12, 57).

In our prayer this week, let's continue to use the Incarnation Colloquy (SE, #109): may we seek the grace to leave behind resentment, selfishness, dishonesty, and fear (see BB, 86) as we try every day "to follow and imitate more closely our Lord, who has just become a human being for me." We are being called to a kingdom of peace (see SE, #91, The Kingdom, First Prelude).

Second Prelude, to Go: Lord Jesus, help me everyday to follow and imitate you more closely, since you have just become a human being – for me.

Meditation 23

Scenes in the Temple

(Lk 2: 22-52)

This passage from Luke contains two neatly balanced scenes from Jesus' childhood, scenes that can stand for the beginning and the end of that childhood. Both scenes take place in the temple in Jerusalem, the center of the worship of Jesus' people. In both scenes, Mary and Joseph have brought Jesus to the temple; in both scenes, Jesus encounters representatives of his Jewish heritage, symbols of the holiness and learning of his people; in both scenes these representatives salute and welcome Jesus into the community of faith. Both scenes involve pain for the mother of Jesus: the pain that Simeon forecasts over the infant Jesus takes definite shape in the incomprehension of his parents when they find their adolescent son in his "Father's house." Both scenes end with summary statements about Jesus continuing to grow in "wisdom" and God's "grace."

These similarities underscore the spiritual connection between the two scenes: they are both steps on the way to Jesus' proclamation of his kind of kingdom. Simeon and Anna are like the shepherds at Jesus' birth in Luke, representatives of the poor and the powerless. Old people are all too often disregarded by various cultures, especially in the United States; and widows like Anna were a class held to be specially under God's protection, in both the Older and the Newer Testaments, because they had no one else to stand up for them. "The kingdom of God belongs to such as these" (Lk 18:16). The "little ones" are always the first to sense Jesus' royalty.

The blessings said over Jesus by the old people in this first scene come true in the second, in which Jesus takes a first step towards embracing the special call from God those blessings presaged. In this second scene, Jesus is twelve, about the age when a Jewish boy has his bar mitzvah, a ceremony during which he is examined in his knowledge of the Law of Moses. Jesus' parents seem to stumble in on their son as he undergoes just such an inquiry by the "teachers" in the Temple: he is passing with flying colors (they "were amazed at his intelligence and his answers"). But his parents barely notice – they are in too much pain as they realize that their son's mission, forecast by Anna and Simeon, is already beginning to take him away from them. The kingdom involves loss.

Recovering people may be able to connect with these scenes in a special way. Many of us may recall that we too were spiritual seekers from early in our lives, perhaps in ways that baffled or distressed our families. Bill W. often suggested that alcoholics were at heart spiritually hungry and thirsty; for instance, he speaks of "alcoholics . . . trying to grope their way toward God in alcohol" (ABSI, #323). As "little ones" we may even have had deep spiritual experiences, only to leave them behind as "childish ways" (1 Cor 13:11); then we detoured into addiction, possibly after some disillusioning experiences with religious people. Recovery, and this retreat as part of our recovery, are opportunities to pick up where we left off so many years ago.

We may also have felt specially blessed at times when we were children; maybe an older woman or man gave us that sense. (Our guide on this retreat – whom we might consult this week – occupies such a role.) And we may, like Jesus, have felt that God was calling us to something special – remember that the grace of the Second Week is "not to be deaf to [God's] call." We may have thought addiction spelled the end of that call; but now, in recovery, we "see how our experience can benefit others" (BB, 84). As recovering alcoholics, we do have a special vocation: "You can help when no one else can" (BB, 89). Pray this week that you may hear God's call to service.

Second Prelude, to Go: Lord Jesus, show me each day how I can use my experiences – even the most painful ones – to benefit others and so to answer the call you gave me even before I was born (see Isaiah 49).

Meditation 24

The Baptism of Jesus

(Mk 1:2-11)

The theme of "call," of vocation, continues this week – God's call of Jesus, and God's call of us, which we are praying for the grace to hear (see SE, #91). Early in the four Gospels – indeed, at the beginning of Mark and John, who do not mention Jesus' childhood – there are descriptions of that moment in Jesus' life when he most clearly sensed his call from God, when he both came to know God's "most holy will" and experienced the "power to carry that out" (compare SE, #109, and the Eleventh Step). This big moment occurred when Jesus was baptized by John.

The scene is rich in symbolism. John is in the desert, and baptizes Jesus in the Jordan: the people of Israel crossed the Jordan into the Promised Land after their long exile in Egypt and the years of wandering in the desert. Jesus is entering a new phase of his life, and is experiencing, like his people before him, "a new freedom and a new happiness" (BB, 83). The "sky rent in two" and the voice from heaven recall God in the pillar of cloud, accompanying God's people on their journey. The dove is an ancient symbol of Israel; the Spirit is the great creative power, which "swept over the waters" at the beginning of everything (Gen 1:2).

But what is most particular for Jesus in this experience is what the voice says: "You are my beloved Son. On you my favor rests." Jesus is a good representative of his people; but beyond that he is also a uniquely loved child of Abba. His hearing of this call will lead him to a ministry in which he will "carry [this] message" to others, and "practice . . . in all [his] affairs" the "principles" that flow from this experience, this sense of "a loving God" (Tradition Two). From the first, he will announce that the Kingdom of God is near, a kingdom founded on just these "principles" – love and service.

In our prayer this week, let's ask to hear this same voice of God, a God that calls us beloved children and invites us to "reform [our] lives" (Mk 1:15) and come into the kingdom to which Jesus calls us. Let us leave the desert behind and cross the "deep river" into the land where we belong.

Second Prelude, to Go: Dear God, let me hear your voice saying to me, too: "You are my beloved child." Then help me to act like it.

Meditation 25

The Temptations of Jesus

(Mt 4:1-11 and Lk 4:1-13)

As often occurs in human life, Jesus' peak experience of God's love at his baptism by John is followed immediately by a desert experience. Jesus may have thought he was entering the Promised Land; instead he is "driven by the Spirit" (Mk 1:12), which came upon him so strongly in the Jordan, to reenact the desert journey of his people. Recovering alcoholics will be able to identify with such a "dry" period; spiritual people in general talk about "prayer and meditation" going "dry," about "times when we can pray only with the greatest exertion of will" (12 X 12, 105, on the Eleventh Step).

Bill W., who knew all about such dark nights, in part because of the depression which plagued him for much of his life, claims that one reason why God sends such "dry" times is so that "new lessons for living [may be] learned, new resources of courage [may be] uncovered" (12 X 12, 105). It is comforting to know that even God's own Son was not exempt from such a painful experience: "All of us, without exception," undergo trials like this (12 X 12, 105). But what "lessons" did Jesus learn from his temptations?

Jesus' temptations in Matthew and Luke have to do with the ministry he is about to begin. After the powerful spiritual experience at his baptism, he might have thought, as Bill W. did just after his life-changing experience, that carrying this message to others was going to be

71

easy. They soon learned otherwise. The purpose of the Temptations is the same as the purpose of the Spiritual Exercises: to help Jesus to choose the way to serve God that God wills, even though that way turns out to be terribly difficult.

These Temptations may seem to be remote from the temptations that ordinary people undergo. After all, Jesus has received the Spirit, and his unique "call" is to be God's anointed, the Messiah. And yet at bottom what the devil tries to beguile Jesus with is exactly what his ancestor the snake used to try to seduce Jesus' human ancestors, Adam and Eve (in Luke, Jesus is called the son of Adam just before the Temptations). As I mentioned above in Meditation Six, the snake wanted Adam and Eve to balk at the Third Step: instead of turning their "will and [their] lives over to the care of God as [they] understood" God, the devil urged them to "be like gods" (Gen 3:5) by misusing their "willpower," by trying "to bombard [their] problems with it instead of attempting to bring it into agreement with God's intention for [them]" (12 X 12, 40).

Jesus succeeds where his ancestors failed: he chooses the way of humility, of trust in God, rather than any of the flashy shortcuts to fame and power that the devil – a "most cunning" (Gen 3:1) marketing genius – dangles before him. Jesus' faith is the more remarkable since he is hungry and tired after his long fast, and lonely – he has not yet made any disciples, since he is still being fine-tuned to carry the message to them. And make no mistake – a big part of the attraction of the devil's offer is that his way is painless. In choosing to serve God on God's terms, Jesus acknowledges that "pain [is] the touchstone of all spiritual progress" (12 X 12, 93-4). God's way for Jesus is going to hurt, and Jesus knows it: Luke ends his account of the Temptations with the remark that the devil will try again at the "right moment" – on the night before the Crucifixion, when Jesus wrestles in the Garden of Gethsemane with the frightening will of Abba for him.

In our prayer this week, let's continue to seek God's will for us, and ask to "follow [Jesus] more closely" (SE, #104) in his following of God's will.

Second Prelude, to Go: Lord Jesus, help me to see thee more clearly, love thee more dearly, and follow thee more nearly, this day and every day.

Meditation 26

Jesus Calls Disciples

(Jn 1:35-51 or Lk 5:1-11)

For the past several weeks, a key word in our prayer has been "call." Ignatius struck this note in the Kingdom Meditation with which we began the Second Week of the Exercises: all this week we are praying to listen to God's call, and so to "follow [Jesus] more closely" (SE, #91, 104). Barely a teenager, Jesus had heard God's call (his encounter with the "teachers" in the Temple); that call was profoundly confirmed at his baptism; and finally the call was purified of any "inordinate attachments" during his ordeal in the desert. Now he is ready to answer the call by carrying the message. In Mark, he does so right after his "forty days" in "the wasteland": "After John's arrest, Jesus appeared in Galilee proclaiming the good news of God: 'This is the time of fulfillment. The reign of God is at hand! Reform your lives and believe in the gospel!'" (Mk 1:13, 14-15; "good news" and "gospel" are the same word in Greek).

But Jesus is not going to do this alone. Maybe this is one of the things he learned in the desert. In any case he will shortly gather disciples around him to help him carry the message of Abba, the loving God. Where does he find them? He "make[s] lifelong friends" "in [his] own community"; they "commence shoulder to shoulder [their] common journey" (BB, 152-3). And now – today – he is calling us to begin the same journey.

How did people back then experience his call? Peter's call, in Luke, gives one version, "in the nature of [a] sudden and spectacular upheaval[ ]" (BB, 569). Jesus works a miracle, Peter senses he is in contact with "Infinite Power and Love" (BB, 56), and the fisherman is instantly crushed by a sudden surge in "the capacity to be honest" (BB, 58) about himself: he cries out, "Leave me, Lord. I am a sinful man" (Lk 5:8). Like so many recovering people, Peter believes "[t]his is the beginning of the end. And so it is: the beginning of the end of his old life, and the beginning of his emergence into a new one" (12 X 12, 26). In acknowledging his powerlessness, Peter has actually taken the first Step on the "common journey" to which Jesus is inviting him. This is why the Spiritual Exercises begin with considerations of our sinfulness; our service will grow most beautifully out of gratitude for having "escape[d] disaster together" (BB, 152).

John the Evangelist's version of the call of the disciples is characteristically gentler and more symbolic: he seems to envision the call as a "spiritual experience" of the "educational variety" (BB, 569). John the Baptist hints to his followers that they should seek out Jesus. Jesus begins their encounter with him by asking them what they want, just as Ignatius suggests that we begin prayer by asking God "for what I want and desire" (SE, #48). What they want is to know where he "lives" (*menein*, "make a home in," a favorite word of John's), in the largest sense – what is the center of his life? He suggests that they "come and see." By living where Jesus lives, they come to believe that he is the Messiah, God's beloved Son; and they in turn carry this message to others, brothers, sisters, friends.

During this week, let's continue to ask to hear God's call, whether that call comes dramatically like Peter's, or as slowly and imperceptibly as the seasons change, like the first disciples' call in John. With the "backing" of "a source of power much greater than [ourselves]," responding generously to God's call "is only a matter of willingness, patience, and labor" (BB, 163).

Second Prelude, to Go: Dear God, whether you shout or whisper, help me to hear you courageously.

The Sermon on the Mount and The Sermon on the Plain

(Mt 5-7 and Lk 6:17-49)

In the Kingdom Meditation, Ignatius pictured a king making an "address . . . to all his subjects," inviting them to join him in an "enterprise" (SE, #93, 95). The king is making a keynote address. In Matthew and Luke, Jesus, too, makes an inaugural address at the beginning of his "enterprise," his mission. Matthew, who thinks of Jesus as, among other things, the new Moses, has Jesus spell out his platform on a mountain; Luke, who particularly admires the appeal of Jesus to the folks near the bottom of the social ladder, has him give it on a plain. But the message in either is pretty similar. It is spelled out in the very first line of Matthew's "Sermon": "How blest are the poor in spirit: the reign of God is theirs" (Mt 5:3).

In other words, the Sermon is about the Kingdom, or "reign," of God; and the point Jesus is making, in verse after verse of the Sermon, is that this reign is utterly different from the way human beings have always thought of power, human or divine. Perhaps the most challenging passage goes like this: "But what I say to you is: offer no resistance to injury. When people strike you on the right cheek, turn and offer them the other. If they want to go to law over your shirt, hand them your coat as well. Should they press you into service for one mile, go with them two miles" (Mt 5:39-41). The proper response to this, then and now, can only be "What an order! I can't go through with it" (BB, 60).

What kind of kingdom is this? One in which all retaliation, even when "justified and reasonable" (12 X 12, 46), is "the dubious luxury of normal [people]" (BB, 66). We are not allowed to mistreat anyone, because we are all children of Abba, "[whose] sun rises on the bad and good, [who] rains on the just and the unjust" (Mt 5:45). Does this sound like a "spiritual perfection" (BB, 60) we can't possibly aspire to? No; Matthew has Jesus say that we are to "be made perfect" as Abba is perfect, but Luke clarifies this by saying that we are to become perfectly what human beings were created to be: "compassionate," as Abba is "compassionate" (Lk 6:36).

Our retreat mentors can help us assess how ready we are at this point to listen to the Call of Jesus the King. Our initial reaction may still well be that of "the average alcoholic, self-centered in the extreme": we may not "care for this prospect" one bit (12 X 12, 24). But in our prayer this week let's remember the very first words of Jesus' ministry: he told those who would answer his call to "Reform your lives and believe in the gospel!" (Mk 1:15).

"Reform" translates *metanoiete,* a key concept in the New Testament; a better translation would be "get ready for 'an entire psychic change'" (BB, xxvii, "The Doctor's Opinion"). The good news, the "gospel," for any Twelve Stepper, is that once we lay hold on such a "change," such a "spiritual awakening," many things become possible "which [at the start] seemed entirely out of reach" (BB, 47).

We sometimes say the Lord's Prayer, part of Matthew's Sermon, at the end of meetings: we ask that the kingdom might come, and in fact it already has – in the compassion and service that have characterized the meeting itself. Let's pray this week that we may "practice [the] principles" of the two Sermons "in all our affairs" (Step Twelve).

Second Prelude, to Go: Dear God, Thy kingdom come, thy will be done on earth, as it is in heaven.

Meditation 28

Healing I – Ephphatha

(Mk 7:31-37)

In the Big Book, Bill W. tells the story – cited above in Meditation 13 – of an early member of A.A.: "a minister's son," he burned out early on "what he thought was an overdose of religious education." Later in life, literally brought to his knees by alcoholism and a host of other woes, he suddenly entered "conscious companionship with his Creator." As a result of this experience, similar to Bill's own life-transforming "spiritual awakening," this man's "alcoholic problem was taken away. . . . Seemingly he could not drink even if he would. God had restored his sanity." Bill's final comment on this story: "What is this but a miracle of healing? Yet its elements are simple. Circumstances made him willing to believe. He humbly offered himself to his Maker – then he knew." Nor was this man's experience unique among early members: "Even so has God restored us all to our right minds. . . [God] has come to all who have honestly sought [God]. When we drew near to [God, God] disclosed [God's] self to us!" (BB, 56-7).

The Gospels are full of stories of Jesus' "miracle[s] of healing." Last week we pondered his carrying of the message in his Great Sermon; but he was more than just a stirring preacher. Contact with him – even being casually touched by him – healed people at the deepest levels of their being. What did these people – "so very ill" in so many ways (BB, 20) – do to be healed? "Circumstances made [them] willing to believe" that Jesus had this remarkable power; they "humbly offered [themselves]," they "drew near to him." And when they did, "he disclosed himself to [them]," he "restored [them] all to [their] right minds," and to "true kinship with [humanity] and God" (12 X 12, 57). As John Dominic Crossan, the New Testament scholar, has pointed out, a large part of Jesus' healing was that he reached out to people who had been ostracized by society, and restored their sense of belonging to the community – precisely the kind of healing that addicts need most.

Since healing was so large a part of who Jesus was, and since recovery from addictions is usually framed in Twelve Step literature as being healed of a disease, we will spend the next three weeks on healing stories from the New Testament. There are of course many of them; I have chosen a few favorites, but you will want to add or substitute stories you like.

The healing story this week is remarkable for its vividness, its concreteness; these features are typical of Mark's Gospel. The man who is healed in this story can neither hear nor speak. The "circumstances" that "made him willing to believe" occurred when friends who could hear about Jesus brought the deaf man to him, and friends who could speak "begged [Jesus] to lay his hand on him." The deaf man "humbly offered himself" to Jesus. The man did not "dr[a]w near to" Jesus, however; instead, Jesus took the initiative and "drew near" to the deaf man by taking him aside, so they could have a moment when it would be just the two of them. Then Jesus literally put his finger on the sore spot: "He put his fingers into the man's ears and, spitting, touched his tongue." Jesus does not withhold himself; he joins his homely spit to the man's spit. He groans; trying to heal people exacts a toll, as anyone who has ever been on a 12th Step call knows. And he says a special word, which Mark, writing in Greek for an audience that spoke only Greek, gives in Jesus' own language, Aramaic, followed by a Greek translation: "Ephphatha! (that is, 'Be opened!')."

"To this man, the revelation was sudden" (BB, 57): "At once the man's ears were opened; he was freed from the impediment, and began to speak plainly" (Mk 7:35). The sequence is interesting here: first the man comes to hear, as newcomers to recovery are urged by old-timers (sometimes quite forcefully) to shut up and listen. Once he can hear, he is (literally) "loosened from his bind," and then he can (literally) "talk straight." Or, in Twelve Step terms, he meets a power that can free him from his "dilemma"; and this power enables him to speak the truth, gives him "the capacity to be honest" (see Big Book, 45, 58). He already had the willingness: he let this stranger stick his fingers into his ears and mouth. Jesus told him to be "open." And, once opened, he could be honest. (See the story "Freedom from Bondage" on H.O.W. – BB, 550.)

This week let us pray that we may grow in love for Jesus, who gets intimately involved with us in our pain so that we can find "a way out" (BB, 17 – *The Way Out* was one of the titles suggested for the Big Book before it was published).

Second Prelude, to Go: Lord Jesus, give me the grace to let you touch the place where I hurt the most, that I may belong to the community of those you have healed.

Meditation 29

Healing II – Parents and Children

(Mk 5:21-24, 35-43; Lk 7:11-17; Mk 9:14-29)

For our second week of reflection on Jesus as a healer who invites us in our turn to carry a healing message to those who still suffer, I have chosen three Gospel stories about parents and children. In the first story, from Mark, a father asks Jesus to heal his little girl. Before Jesus gets to the man's house, the little girl dies, but even death is not too much for the "Infinite Power and Love" (BB, 56) that took flesh in Jesus.

The story from Luke bears this out: here a mother has lost her only son. No one even asks Jesus to do something about her loss – he is so "moved with pity" that he takes the initiative. Perhaps Jesus is thinking ahead to what his own mother will have to go through when his preaching of a kingdom of peace gets him killed. Finally, Mark tells the wrenching story of a man with an epileptic son; like most of us, the man has some faith, but is not sure that he has enough. In anguish, he cries out, "I do believe! Help my lack of trust!" (literally "I believe! Help my un-belief!"). His honesty wins the day: "God does not make too hard terms with those who seek [God]" (BB, 46).

I chose these stories because they depict Jesus reaching out to people in what is probably the worst circumstance that human beings can undergo – the threat of the loss of their child. Bill W. mentions this as a great test of faith, of our belief in the power of prayer: "[I]t's not strange that lots of us have had our day at defying God . . . .

We prayed for healthy children, and were presented with sick ones, or none at all. . . . Loved ones . . . were taken from us by so-called acts of God. . . . 'Damn this faith business!' we said" (12 X 12, 31; Bill and his wife Lois were unable to have children, and were turned down for adoption because of Bill's drinking).

In prayer this week, pay special attention to what Jesus does with each sick, or dead, child. Mark uses the same words to describe Jesus' gestures with the daughter of Jairus and with the epileptic boy: Jesus takes them both by the hand and tells them, or helps them, to get up. With the son of the widow of Naim, he touches the bier; but he uses the same word as in Mark to tell the young man to "get up."

Both the touching and the command are significant: dead bodies are non-kosher, and touching them brings social defilement. And what we call epilepsy, Jesus' contemporaries thought of as possession by a devil, which would make the epileptic boy in Mark 9 an object of horror to most people then. Yet Jesus is not afraid to touch the untouchable; and this is life-giving. In fact, the word for "get up," in all three cases, is also one of the words used for Jesus' resurrection from the dead. Healing for Jesus is a matter of life and death; and because of the power that Jesus draws from Abba, life wins.

In our prayer this week, then, let us be grateful for the ways God has touched our lives and raised us up. With remarkable understatement, Bill W. notes that "[a]n alcoholic in his cups is an unlovely creature" (BB, 16). And yet people reached out hands to us even when we were "unlovely"; raised to our feet, we "march[ed] on" with them (BB, 153). As we march on, let's continue to ask how we can "follow [Jesus] more closely" (SE, #104) by reaching out to and raising up "the alcoholic who still suffers" (Tradition Five).

Second Prelude, to Go: Dear God, thanks for lifting me to my feet. Now help me to take steps to carry the message to those who still suffer.

Meditation 30

Healing III – Jesus and Women

(Mk 5:25-34; Lk 8:1-3)

For our last week of meditation on Jesus as Healer, I have chosen two passages that portray Jesus as a healer of women. Luke makes a summary statement of the fact: some of the people who "accompanied" Jesus as he carried the message were women whom he had "cured" of "maladies" (Lk 8:1, 2). The word for "cured" is the Greek root from which we get "therapy"; "maladies" literally means "strengthless spirits." What Jesus healed in these women – some of them upper class women, apparently – was their powerlessness. The Spirit Jesus gives is a spirit of power; in Luke the two words are practically synonymous.

Mark tells a story (surrounded by the story of Jairus' daughter) of a particular woman whom Jesus heals. As I stressed last week, a key element in the story of the little girl is that Jesus touches her; just so, a key element in the story of the woman is that she touches him. Just like the little girl, the woman is non-kosher, not to be touched, because she has a woman's physical problem: chronic menstruation. This means she has spent twelve years outside the community. And she is doubly disadvantaged, as a chronically ill woman, and as a woman in a patriarchal culture. "Circumstances made [her] willing to believe" (BB, 57): "She had heard about Jesus" (Mk 5:27). She was braver, or more desperate, than some of the untouchable men who had asked Jesus to heal them: leprous men, for example, asked Jesus to heal them, but did not touch him.

She takes the risk of touching first, without asking for permission.

The point of Jesus' making a scene is "not to embarrass her," of course, but so that the message can be proclaimed loud and clear. In the kingdom that he is heralding, everybody will be touchable, and necessarily so, because to touch is to find faith and hope, to touch is to heal and be healed. From Jesus the woman has received "healing *power*" (the word Luke often uses for the Spirit); she need no longer be lost in the crowd – she can resume "all normal activities," including "civic duties" (BB, 131). Perhaps she joined the women who "accompanied" Jesus on his way.

Alcoholic men as well as alcoholic women – and people with chronic illnesses as well – can identify with this woman's quest for healing, and especially with her isolation: "The less people tolerated us [while we were drinking], the more we withdrew from society, from life itself" (BB, 151). Like this woman, alcoholic women have always faced more of a stigma than alcoholic men because of cultural beliefs about female drinking. This has often made it more difficult for women to reach out for help with an addiction. But it also makes recovery that much more of a relief when a woman finds it: after attending her first meeting, on a pass from a sanitarium, one of the first women members of A.A. said to a hard-drinking friend, a fellow inmate, "Grenny, we're not alone any more" (see BB, 228).

This week, let's continue to ask to follow Jesus, a king who lets himself be touched by all who want what he has. And let us pray that, in our service, people may find us touchable, and not "Holier Than Thou" (BB, 18).

Second Prelude, to Go: Lord Jesus, give me the grace to be touched by other people's pain, as you touched, and were touched by, my pain.

Meditation 31

Jesus and Parables

(Mt 13)

Most of the great spiritual teachers, and especially the great rabbis, have used stories to carry their message, and Jesus was no exception. In fact, one of his favorite teaching tools was the parable; the Gospels are studded with them. In Matthew's Gospel, a set of parables is collected in Chapter 13: all of them have to do with the kingdom, the "reign," of God – the Greek word for kingdom occurs twelve times in this chapter.

What is the kingdom of Abba like, then, according to Jesus? One thing is very clear from these parables: the kingdom contains all kinds of people, of "many political, economic, [and] social backgrounds . . . people who normally would not mix" (BB, 17). Jesus says, "The reign of God is . . . like a dragnet thrown into the lake, which collected all sorts of things" (Mt 13:47). Naturally, as members of such a motley fellowship, we are tempted to want to impose some kind of order on this messy catch. But we don't get to sort them out, e.g., into those favorite human categories "good" (= "like me") and "bad" (= "different"). Bill insists that we aren't supposed to "confess[ ] the sins of other people. Everybody ha[s] to confess [their] own" (12 X 12, 57). Only God, who is far more loving than we are, and far more clever about getting usefulness out of people we consider useless, gets to decide what is "worthwhile" and what is "useless."

The kingdom of God is also like mustard seed and yeast (Mt 13:31-33). It starts very small, but it grows very large; and it does so naturally, organically, without our needing to fuss about it. This can comfort us when we feel "jittery and alone" on our spiritual path: "Thus we grow" (BB, 163, 162), like seed casually thrown. Thomas Aquinas put it this way: *Bonum est diffusivum sibi,* "The Good spreads itself, pours itself all over." Good news travels fast, and far. Bill W. quoted the song of the angels at Jesus' birth to describe the ever-spreading effect of his sponsor Ebby's 12th Step of him: "Each day my friend's simple talk in our kitchen multiplies itself in a widening circle of peace on earth and good will to men [and women]" (BB, 16). Where peace and grace are, there is the kingdom of God.

Finally, the kingdom is like a treasure, or "one really valuable pearl" (Mt 13:44-46). If you have found this treasure, it only makes sense to give all you have for it. As the great mystical love poem in the Bible, the Song of Songs, puts it, "Were you to offer all you own to purchase love, you would be roundly mocked" (8:7) – "mocked" because love is beyond any price. Bill uses a similar image to describe recovery: "Like a gaunt prospector, belt drawn in over the last ounce of food, our pick struck gold. . . . [we have] barely scratched a limitless lode which will pay dividends only if [we] mine [ ] it for the rest of [our] li[v]e[s] and insist[ ] on giving away the entire product" (BB, 128-9). In the context of the Second Week, the priceless pearl is our Call from God, who created us to follow Jesus by serving God and our fellows (see 7th Step Prayer, BB, 76) as only we uniquely can.

Stories are also important in the Twelve Step fellowships. "Our stories" – "what we used to be like, what happened, and what we are like now" (BB, 58) – are the principal way in which we carry the message of recovery.

Addicts – and those who love addicts – "don't always care for people who lecture us" (BB, 121; from the chapter "To Wives"). But addicts, perhaps even more than other people, "care for people" who share the stories of their lives. Our story is our treasure, our pearl; "frequently it is almost the only [asset]" we have (BB, 124). Still, when, like Ebby and Bill, we get together and trade our "assets," great spiritual power is released: "Now and then we may be granted a glimpse of that ultimate reality which is God's kingdom" (12 X 12, 98, on Step Eleven).

In our prayer this week, let's keep coming back to two phrases from the Lord's Prayer, both of which say the same thing: "Thy kingdom come, Thy will be done on earth as it is in heaven."

Second Prelude, to Go: Dear God, Thy kingdom come, Thy will be done on earth as it is in heaven.

Meditation 32

The Transfiguration of Jesus

(Lk 9:28-36)

Matthew, Mark, and Luke all describe this incident: partway through Jesus' ministry, he was granted a peak experience. So powerful was this experience that it changed him, not just inside, but even on the outside. Luke uses an unusual phrase to describe it: Jesus "shone like a star." A Voice repeats, more or less, what the Voice said at Jesus' first great experience of God's Call, his baptism by John in the Jordan: Jesus is Abba's Beloved Son.

What's different about this occasion is that Jesus is no longer alone. He has brought his three closest disciples with him. And they need to share this experience, because Jesus has assured them, just before this Transfiguration, that he is going to die a miserable, shameful death. *That's* the kind of King he really is, that's the kind of Kingdom of which they are early members. The disciples hate this notion. They don't want this to happen to their Master, of course, but they also have had a rather different vision of what is coming to them as Important People in the Kingdom. They have been thinking about thrones, not execution. Jesus' sudden "shining" restores their faith – for a while. In the long run, of course, they will have to grasp that Jesus is God's beloved precisely because he is willing to give his life if God's will requires it.

Even at this supremely glorious moment in Jesus' life, the reality of the impending crucifixion is not far away. Moses and Elijah are also present at the Transfiguration;

representatives of the faith of Jesus' people, they give their blessing to Jesus. But in Luke these figures from the Hebrew Scriptures speak of Jesus' "passage" – literally his "exodus" – which he is going to "fulfill in Jerusalem." Like his people escaping from slavery to Pharaoh, Jesus, when he finishes his journey by arriving in Jerusalem, will be seeking a "way out" (this is what "exodus" means in Greek). The central paradox of the story of Jesus is that his inglorious "way out" of life is his glorious way home to Abba, his "royal" road: before the resurrection must come the passion. The "way out" of "the bondage of self" (Third Step Prayer) is self-giving, for Jesus and for those who would follow him.

Ignatius was deeply in tune with this truth. Passages in the Kingdom Meditation, at the beginning of this Second Week, foreshadow it: King Jesus says there, "whoever wishes to join me in this enterprise must be willing to labor with me, that by following me in suffering, [they] may follow me in glory" (SE, #95). It also lies at the heart of his reflections on choice of a way of life (see Meditations 35-37 below). Bill W. cites similar qualities when he invites us to pass on what we have received in recovery: what is needed for 12th Step work is "willingness, patience [from the Latin *patior*, "suffer"] and labor" (BB, 163).

As we go through this Week, as we try to deepen our commitment as disciples of Jesus, we need to look honestly at the price. Can we believe that, even in our suffering, we remain loved children of God? Can we trust that our suffering is "unaccountably transform[ing]" us into something radiant (12 X 12, 28, on Step Two), something "like a star"? If you "balk" at this, if your response is "What an order! I can't go through with it!" (BB, 58, 60), pray for the grace to "want to want" God's will for you (BB, 109).

Second Prelude, to Go: Dear God, make your grace shine forth from me, so that my experience, however painful, may benefit others.

Note on the Timing of the "Election"

At some point in the middle of this Second Week, you may want to take a look at Meditations 35-37, below. As you may remember, the purpose of the Spiritual Exercises is to become free enough of "inordinate attachment" to make good decisions about how we can best serve God with our lives (SE, #21). Ignatius assumes that, "if we are painstaking" about the Exercises of the Second Week, we will be more or less ready to make those decisions "before we are halfway through" this Week and through the Exercises as a whole (BB, 83). Meditations 35-37 deal with some specific considerations Ignatius offers us to help with these big life decisions. If you are fortunate enough to be making the Exercises with a spiritual guide, you should consult them about when to take up these Meditations: "people of very high spiritual development almost always insist on checking with friends or spiritual advisers the guidance they feel they have received from God," and so should anyone else who is making "progress" on a spiritual path (12 X 12, 60; BB, 62).

The idea here is that at a certain point in the Second Week you will feel like you have come to know Jesus well enough to make a decision to follow him. Meditations 35-37 help you to flesh out the details of exactly how you will turn your will and your life over to the care of Abba, the God of Jesus. What's the best way for you to help make God's kingdom come? After you make this small detour, pick up the Meditations of the Second Week wherever you left off. But the rest of the Week may feel a little different – "sometimes a very great [effect is] felt at once" (BB, 63). For you have taken a very profound Third Step now; and once you have "abandon[ed] [yourself] utterly" (BB, 63)

to Abba, you are more a disciple of Jesus than you have
ever been.

Meditation 33

Jesus Feeds the People

(Mt 14:13-21)

This familiar story encapsulates the theme of all our meditations during this Second Week: it is about discipleship. The key moment comes when Jesus, pitying the crowd that has followed him into the desert, tells his disciples, "Give them something to eat yourselves" (Mt 14:16). He could have simply taken care of the problem himself, but he wants to involve his disciples, to let them know that, because of the "spiritual awakening" they have experienced with him, they can feed people in the same way he does.

Their reaction is understandable: "We have nothing here." They are probably saying to themselves, "We are jittery and alone. We couldn't do that." True, there's a little bit of food, but as Simon Peter worriedly points out in John's version of this story, "[W]hat good is that for so many?" (Jn 6:8). Jesus tells them to start the meeting anyway; so the disciples tell the crowd to sit down in an orderly way. Jesus does some Eleventh Step work, in the form of a Jewish blessing prayer over the bread and fish. The disciples have enough faith to start passing out the food; perhaps they recall that they have "tapped a source of power much greater than" themselves. In any case, they demonstrate "willingness, patience and labor" (BB, 163). What happens? "It works – it really does" (BB, 88): "All those present ate their fill" (Mt 13:20).

One of the principles that followers of Jesus are to practice is this: if we run into hungry people, we ought to feed them. Jesus has assured us that one of the questions on the Final Exam will be, "Did you feed the hungry?" (see Mt 25:31-46 for *all* the questions). But bread is also a symbol for wisdom, for God's word, for the Message that we are supposed to carry. In John's Gospel, Jesus gives a sermon after the Feeding of the Crowd in which he compares the bread he has given them both to God's word in general and to Himself as God's ultimate Word: we need to feed on both if we are going to follow Jesus. And we particularly need to feed on both if we are in our turn going to feed other people, as the disciples of Jesus do – "obviously you cannot transmit something you haven't got" (BB, 164).

So during this week, let us take our spiritual hunger and thirst to the One who can give us all we need, not just for ourselves, but for crowds of people who are still lost in the desert. And let us continue to ask that we may more deeply understand God's call to discipleship. Like Jesus, we are being invited by God to feed people with our lives, our stories, our "word" – the "word" we are, more than the words we speak. In responding to that call, we "will know what it means to give of [ourselves] that others may survive and rediscover life. [We] will learn the full meaning of 'Love thy neighbor as thyself'" (BB, 153).

Second Prelude, to Go: Dear God, make of my life and of all your other gifts to me food for the hungry in spirit.

Meditation 34

Walking on the Sea

(Mt 14:22-33)

One of Bill W.'s favorite sets of images for alcohol, alcoholism, and recovery revolves around the ocean, shipwreck, and rescue. Such an image comes early in the Big Book, right after Bill's personal story: "We are like the passengers of a great liner the moment after rescue from shipwreck when camaraderie, joyousness and democracy pervade the vessel from steerage to Captain's table. Unlike the feelings of the ship's passengers, however, our joy in escape from disaster does not subside as we go our individual ways. The feeling of having shared in a common peril is one element in the powerful cement which binds us. But that in itself would never have held us together as we are now joined. The tremendous fact for every one of us is that we have discovered a common solution" (BB, 17).

Towards the end of the first, theoretical part of the Big Book, Bill varies this metaphor: "Our hope is that when this chip of a book is launched on the world tide of alcoholism, defeated drinkers will seize upon it, to follow its suggestions" (BB, 153). Here the Big Book functions as a kind of crude life-preserver, rescuing the drowning.

It's no surprise that this kind of image for deadly drinking would occur to Bill. Alcoholics are in the hellish position of Coleridge's Ancient Mariner: "Water, water everywhere/Nor any drop to drink." We are dying of thirst and drowning, simultaneously, because alcohol, a liquid, actually makes people thirstier. Perhaps Bill was also thinking of a ship like the *Titanic,* it's part of the legend of that ill-fated vessel that people went from an elegant party with glamorous drinking to watery death, still in evening clothes, a few hours later, a foreshortened version of many an alcoholic's course.

How to "escape from" this disaster? The solution that Jesus offers in this week's Gospel passage made the disciples' jaws drop: when you're drowning, stand up on the waves and start taking steps. Terror is a natural reaction to such a mind-boggling, audacious proposal. But Peter, whom Jesus loved deeply for his impetuosity – everything Peter thought and felt went straight to his mouth – hears Jesus' call to courage. People need courage to change the things they can. And Peter does all right for a moment or two, emboldened by his Second Step.

But then he falls into the hole between Steps Two and Three. Being healed of his sinfulness by Jesus is one thing, but turning over his *life,* especially when the wind is this strong – that's another story. As Jesus points out to him, he gets into trouble because he "falter[s]" – the word in Greek means "is of two minds." At a moment when single-mindedness is essential, Peter has gotten himself into a "dilemma" (which literally means being frozen between two choices). Lack of power, that is his dilemma (BB, 45; see also "terrible dilemma" on 28). As Bill put it, with considerable understatement, "To be doomed to an alcoholic death" – death by drowning – "or to live on a spiritual basis are not always easy alternatives to face" (BB, 44).

Ignatius experienced a similar ordeal. Soon after his conversion, when he was still trying to bombard his spiritual problems with willpower (12 X 12, 40), "a forceful thought came to trouble him by pointing out the hardships of his life, like a voice within his soul, 'How will you be able to endure this life for the seventy years you have to live?'" (*SE and Selected Works*, ed. Ganss, 76). Ignatius had become a "religious enthusiast" (BB, 128), fasting and doing terrific penances; he started to sink at the idea that this would go on for the rest of his life. Alcoholics, faced with the prospect of walking above the sea of alcohol for the remainder of their days, may well sink, too.

"There is a solution" (title of BB, Ch. 2). As Ignatius did, we recall that the spiritual life, like life in general, comes one day at a time. And having "faltered" at Step Three, like Peter we go back to Step One and shout out our powerlessness: "Lord, save me!" (Mt 13:30). And a hand is stretched out to raise us up. "We trust infinite God rather than our finite selves" (BB, 68). In our prayer this week, let's continue to ask God to increase our faith so that we can answer God's call with generosity.

Second Prelude, to Go: Dear God, in your great power help my powerlessness. Filled with your strength, I will follow you *today*.

Note on The Election after SE, #135

As I mentioned above, Ignatius suggests that retreatants take some time out somewhere around the middle of the Second Week to consider just what they will do with their lives in order to make a grateful return to Jesus for the gifts of their conversion. For recovering people, the matter at issue can be put like this: in exactly what way can we best work our Twelfth Step? In exactly what way can we best follow Jesus, whom we have come to know better and love well during this Week? Perhaps in consultation with your retreat guide, you have decided that now is the right moment for you to do this.

The word that is used for this choice in the Exercises is "the election," a literal rendering of the Spanish word for "choice." Some retreatants may be young, and so on the verge of their big choices. And some may be "reborn" through recovery (BB, 63), and so in a position to choose afresh. And finally, as Ignatius points out, in some cases retreatants will be making the Exercises long after they have made all or most of their big life choices, and there may be no reason to change those choices. In this instance they choose the same things again – relationships, career, and so on – but in a less compulsive, freer, more grateful way.

The "primary purpose" of the Exercises as a whole is to expedite this "election." But at this moment, when we are closely examining life choices, Ignatius provides three particular meditations to help to clarify the process of choice, and to enhance the degree of freedom to do God's will that we have reached up to this point. My version of those three meditations follows (Meditations 35, 36, and 37).

Meditation 35

The Two Standards

(SE, #136 ff.)

With this meditation, we return to some of the ideas of the Kingdom Meditation, which prefaces the Second Week. There Ignatius contrasted an ordinary earthly king – a decent guy, but no Messiah – with Jesus the King. Ignatius' point was that Jesus' kingdom was, in Jesus' words to Pilate, the representative of the Roman Empire, "not of this world" (Jn 18:36). As we have seen from time to time during the Meditations of this Week, Jesus' life, from its very beginning, and his words and actions, constantly point to a new vision of God's reign, in which everyone is welcome, and in which "service," not "power," is the password. His astonishing vision was so alien to the expectations of his contemporaries that even his closest friends, his disciples, were baffled by it, and frequently humored him without really believing in this "kingdom" of his.

In the meditation on Two Standards, Ignatius once again has a dual comparison of Jesus and another Ruler. But this time the Other is Evil – call him King Addiction, if you want. The Other is everything that goes wrong in the world, everything that follows from "this brave philosophy, wherein each [one] plays God." What follows is that "everywhere . . . people [are] filled with anger and fear, society [is] breaking up into warring fragments. . . . The philosophy of self-sufficiency . . . is a bone-crushing juggernaut whose final achievement is ruin" (12 X 12, 37; published in 1953, shortly after the detonation of the first

H-bomb). The Other is the embodiment of this "brave philosophy."

The title of this meditation, the Two Standards, is another mildly stilted translation from the Spanish. The word for "standard" is *bandera*, which means "flag," or "pennant," or "banner." Ignatius asks us to imagine what appears on the flag of the Other – a dollar sign? a mushroom cloud? a huge "I"? What appears on the flag of Jesus the King, of course, is a simple cross (see the Third Week, below).

Ignatius paints vivid contrasting scenes both of the Other, "seated on a great throne" (SE, #140), and of Jesus, "standing in a lowly place in a great plain about the region of Jerusalem" (SE, #144). Taking a note from St. Luke's Sermon on the Plain (see Meditation 27), Ignatius stresses Jesus' humility – he is down-to-earth, he is on our level. Ignatius also underscores that Jesus welcomes all to his kingdom – the message is carried "to all people, no matter what their state or condition" (SE, #145). But the key to this Exercise is in the "address[es]" (*sermon* in Spanish) that Jesus and the Other deliver to their followers.

If we buy the notion that "[o]ur liquor was but a symptom," of what is "our liquor" a symptom (BB, 64)? How exactly do people get hooked into addictive behavior (Ignatius speaks of "snares" and "chains")? The "address" of the Other "get[s] down to causes and conditions" (BB, 64).

Curiously, Ignatius speaks here of "steps" (*escalones*) – "steps" that lead down to addiction, and, later in this meditation, "steps" that lead up to "spiritual progress." The steps that lead down are three (SE, #142): the first is wealth, or what the Sixth Tradition warns against as "money" and "property." The problem with these things is that they tend to "divert us from our primary purpose" as human beings, which, as the First Principle reminded us, is "to praise, reverence, and serve God" (SE, #23). Then, too, a problem with money is that we may seek it, not for what we can do with it, but because it can make us feel important: so the second step downward is greed for "honor," or what the Sixth Tradition calls "prestige." Bill W. comments on the problems caused by an addictive desire for this commodity: "When an individual's desire for prestige becomes uncontrollable, whether in the sewing circle or at the international conference table, other people suffer and often revolt" (12 X 12, 44).

The third and final step down is pride, which "heads the procession" of "major human failings" (12 X 12, 48). In short, if we take a good look at the flag of the Other, we see that his come-on is the old, tired lie of addiction: if I only have enough things, everyone will admire me, and then I can feel good about myself. For alcoholics specifically, this is how it works: "For thousands of years we have been demanding more than our share of security, prestige, and romance. When we seemed to be succeeding, we drank to dream still greater dreams. When we were frustrated, even in part, we drank to forget. Never was there enough of what we thought we wanted" (12 X 12, 71).

Just after the passage just quoted, Bill diagnoses the basic problem of alcoholics, of which "liquor [is] but a symptom": "In all these strivings, so many of them well-intentioned, our crippling handicap had been our lack of humility." Ignatius would agree completely: Christ's "address" (SE, #146) leads straight to "humility" – that is the third step on the upward path. The first step is, as against wealth, "poverty" – either the "poverty in spirit" of the First Beatitude, a condition attained by any genuine First Step, or even "actual poverty," if that is God's will. A.A. by its Traditions has "elected" such poverty from early in its history, the better to achieve its "primary purpose."

The second upward step, as against honors, is "insults or contempt." Few people aspire to being alcoholics; and while those of us who have embraced the disease concept are not ashamed of our condition, there will probably always be plenty of people, including those very close to us, who will dismiss that concept as a contemptible alibi. Can we nevertheless "seek rather. . . to understand, than to be understood" (12 X 12, 99, quoting the prayer of St. Francis of Assisi)? And – again – the third step up is humility. So important is this virtue in the practice of the Twelve Steps that a whole Step (Seven) is devoted to it: "[This] is where we make the change in our attitude which permits us, with humility as our guide, to move out from ourselves toward others and toward God" (12 X 12, 76).

As we pray over the Two Flags this week, let's keep in mind that the purpose here is not to get humble in our rooms; the purpose of this Meditation, like the purpose of the Seventh Step, is to help us to let go of "every single defect of character that stands in the way of my usefulness to you [God] and to my fellows" (Seventh Step Prayer, BB, 76). Or, as Jesus puts it in his "address," we should desire humility because we "seek to help all . . . by attracting them" (SE, #146; Ignatius describes Jesus in this meditation as "beautiful and attractive," SE, #144). "Without [humility], [A.A. members have found that] they cannot live to much useful purpose" (12 X 12, 70). Let us pray this week, in the words of the Third Step Prayer, that God will "build with [us] and do with [us] as [God wills]" (BB, 63).

Second Prelude, to Go: "God, I offer myself to thee – to build with me and to do with me as Thou wilt. Relieve me of the bondage of self, that I may better do Thy will" (from the Third Step Prayer – BB, 63).

Meditation 36

Three Kinds of People

(SE, #149 ff.)

This is the second meditation Ignatius provides to help us to "choose [literally, "embrace," "hug,"] that which is better." The set-up here is straightforward: all the "people" in this meditation have gotten hold of some money, "but not entirely as they should have." Now they find themselves "attached" to it, while at the same time they want to rid "themselves of the burden" of it, since it interferes with their "primary purpose," that is, serving God and others. Since Ignatius uses "money" as a symbol for all the material things to which people become attached – all of which money can buy, after all – you might want to modify this meditation by inserting whatever attachments you are burdened with, whatever makes you less free to choose the best way for you to serve God.

The fact that the "money" in this meditation was ill-gotten is another way to say that some life choices you have made arose from compulsions you are only now becoming fully aware of. For instance, you became a social worker out of idealism, but also – you now see – because your family was a mess, yet no one in it was allowed to say so. As Bill W. notes, mixed motives "permeate[ ] human affairs from top to bottom" (12 X 12, 94).

The point of this meditation is the reaction of the Three Kinds of People to their dawning awareness of how attached they are. After they take a First Step – "I am powerless over my attachment to X" – then what? The First

Kind of People, having gotten to the First Step, stop dead there; they procrastinate. "They would like to rid themselves of the attachment . . . in order to find peace [a 12-Stepper would say "serenity"] in God our Lord," but they never take any further steps in that direction (SE, #153). They die without knowing "a new freedom and a new happiness" (BB, 83). Many alcoholics – probably most alcoholics – never find permanent recovery, even though they sense at some level that they are attached to alcohol.

The Second Kind of People want to have their cake and eat it: "[t]hey want to rid themselves of the attachment, but they wish to do so in such a way that they retain what they have acquired." For alcoholics, this takes the form of "the great obsession of every abnormal drinker" – "[t]he idea that somehow, someday [they] will control and enjoy [their] drinking." In other words, the Second Kind of Drunk makes "countless vain attempts to drink like other people" (BB, 30). These People know at some level that they're addicted, but they keep using because they don't *want* to be addicted. Unlike the First Kind, this Kind does something, but they "misuse . . . willpower" (12 X 12, 40) by throwing it at their addiction. As Ignatius notes, they want God to do their will (SE, #154), rather than saying "[God's] will, not mine, be done" (12 X 12, 41).

The Third Kind of People took me by surprise when I first did this Exercise. I suspect it takes most people aback: that is the point of this meditation. We might assume – especially if we are alcoholics, who have been trying to change the things we can't by uselessly throwing willpower at them – that the Third Kind works like mad trying to "remove all these defects of character" (Sixth Step). But that is not what Ignatius says, or what the Sixth and Seventh Step call for. The Third Kind of People "seek only to will and not will as God our Lord inspires them, and as seems better for the service and praise of the Divine Majesty. . . . They will make efforts neither to want that [i.e., to have the attachment removed], nor anything else, unless the service of God our Lord alone moves them to do so. As a result, the desire to be better able to serve God our Lord will be the cause of their accepting anything or relinquishing it" (SE, #155).

We have gotten, by a different road, to the same place that we reached in the Meditation on the Two Standards: we *humbly* ask God to remove our defects of character, leaving it to God to decide which defects "stand in the way of our usefulness to [God] and to our fellows" (Seventh Step Prayer, BB, 76). The reason why the Serenity Prayer is so popular among 12 Steppers is that it reminds them that it takes wisdom to know when to use willpower to change things, and when to bow gracefully to the inevitable. The sign that their conscious contact with God is improving is their increasing readiness to pray "only for knowledge of [God's] will for us and the power to carry that out" (Eleventh Step). This is also the hallmark of the Third Kind of People. Let us ask to follow Jesus in detachment this week, that we may be of greater service to the God who has liberated us "from a seemingly hopeless state of mind and body" (Foreword to the First Edition, BB, xiii).

Second Prelude, to Go: Lord Jesus, help me to let go of what you think doesn't help.

Three Degrees of Humility

(SE, #165-167)

This is the third and final Exercise that St. Ignatius provides to help us to make the freest life-choices we can. Just as in the previous two meditations, humility is the crucial virtue; humility is the identifying trait of the Kingdom of God as Jesus proclaimed it. The Shakers, an American Christian group that flourished in the nineteenth century, carried this message in a much-loved hymn of theirs: "'Tis the gift to be simple/'Tis the gift to be free/'Tis the gift to come down where we ought to be/ And when we find ourselves in the place just right/'Twill be in the valley of love and delight."

In this meditation Ignatius describes three "types" of humility ("types" is my translation of *maneras*, traditionally translated "degrees," since Ignatius ranks them from lower to higher). The first two degrees have parallels in Bill W.'s analysis of Step Seven. He speaks of "some degree of humility" without which "no alcoholic can stay sober at all" (12 X 12, 70). It takes humility to acknowledge that "where we ought to be" is a room full of alcoholics. This roughly corresponds to Ignatius's First Degree of Humility, which says that "not even were I made lord of all creation, or to save my life here on earth" (SE, #165), would I forget what God has done for me. For an addict, this is almost a truism; if I forget "what [I] used to be like" and "what happened," (BB, 58), if I relapse into active addiction, it won't matter that I have "gain[ed] the whole

world" – I will have "destroyed [my]self in the process"
(Mt 16:26). To lose this fundamental humility is "infinitely
grave" (BB, 66) for an alcoholic, because it is the key to
continued recovery.

Bill W. later speaks of another "degree of humility":
this goes beyond the humility necessary to "banish" the
"deadly obsession" with our primary addiction, and gives
us "hope . . . respecting any other problem we could possibly have," and particularly hope for "the removal of our
other shortcomings" (12 X 12, 76). In other words, there's
a humility of the First Step, which is basic to sobriety; and
then there is the humility of the Seventh Step, which ac-
cepts what God does in our lives to "remove every single
defect of character that stands in the way of my usefulness
to [God] and to my fellows" (Seventh Step Prayer, BB,
76).

Ignatius' Second Degree of Humility also speaks of
"service of God our Lord." In addition, he invokes the detachment of the First Principle and Foundation: "[M]y attitude of mind is such that I neither desire nor am I
inclined to have riches rather than poverty, to seek honor
rather than dishonor, to desire a long life rather than a
short life" (SE, #166). Acceptance is the key here: I am
willing humbly to accept whatever God sends, if that is
how I can best serve God. Those defects of character that
prevent me from serving well will be removed, and the removal will very likely hurt; on the other hand, defects of
character that embarrass me, yet somehow help other people, will probably stay, since they are somehow useful. And
that's OK with us.

At this point we are pretty much where we were at
the end of last week's meditation, with the Third Kind of
People, who wait on God's will. But with the Third Degree
of Humility, we make a quantum leap, not so much to dif-

ferent behavior on our part, as to a different motivation for our behavior, and especially for our life-choices. Jesus is not specifically mentioned in the meditation on Three Kinds of People; but Jesus is the focus of the Third Degree of Humility, as he is of the Second Week. His disciples may not have grasped, at least during his lifetime, the kind of kingdom he was announcing; but we who have been meditating on just this fact for weeks now surely have gotten the point. The Third Degree of Humility suggests the title of that medieval classic of spirituality, *The Imitation of Christ*: if we reach this Degree, we will leave "indifference" behind, and actively choose to follow Jesus, to become a citizen of his kingdom, knowing that this will mean "poverty" rather than "money" and "property," "insults" rather than "prestige" (SE, #167 and the Sixth Tradition). Why? Not because that will make people admire us, or because ethically this is the best thing to do; but because "Christ was treated [this way] before [us]."

Even here, Ignatius is prudent; we make these noble choices so that God can be served, not to impress other people or ourselves. And the motivation is not masochism; it is love and gratitude. We began this Week praying for "the grace" to be "prompt and diligent to accomplish [God's] most holy will" (SE, #91). As we shall see in the Third Week, the "will" of God for God's own Son was profoundly difficult. The Third Degree of Humility says in essence this: if God's will was good enough for Jesus, whom we are spending this week getting to know, love, and follow, it's good enough for us. Let us pray this week that we will make – or re-make – our life-choices by using these "principles" to evaluate "all our affairs."

Second Prelude, to Go: Lord Jesus, help me to choose what you chose, because you chose it.

✣

Third Week

With the help of your retreat guides, you have decided it's
time to move on to the next week. The purpose of the
Third Week is to subject the "spiritual principle[s]" we
have so far learned, and the life-choices we have made
during the Second Week, to a "major test": Will "the kind
of dependence" on God's will that we have "learned in
A.A." – and embraced more deeply during this retreat –
"carry [us] through" (12 X 12, 38)? We have perhaps
taken a deeper Third Step, become more whole-heartedly
a disciple of Jesus. Can we follow him to the fearful out-
come to which his choices brought him, to the ultimate
test of his "dependence" on Abba, to whom he had
turned over his will and his life?

The grace we asked for in the Second Week was to
know, love, and follow Jesus. This week we will try to follow him to the end of his life. So the graces Ignatius bids
us ask for this Week are "sorrow" and "compassion" for
Jesus in "His suffering" (SE, #193). We will be returning,
with a deeper sense of who Jesus is for us, to the Colloquy
of the First Week, where we asked ourselves, before Jesus
on the cross, what we were going to do for Christ. And
one of the things we can do for Christ is to strive to let go
of our human resentments and fears which, as we shall
see, subjected him to the greatest temptation of his life:
could he "match calamity with serenity" (BB, 68), could

he stay true to his vision of a peaceful Kingdom, without retaliating, even when the Powerful, when the Angry and the Fearful, came for him? During this week, let us pray, in the words of Isaiah, that "by his wounds" we may be "healed" (Is 53:5).

Meditation 38

Jesus Washes the Feet of His Disciples

(Jn 13:1-17)

This scene takes place at the Last Supper, the night before Jesus died. John's opening is very solemn: Jesus knows that this is the time for him to go home to Abba; before he goes, he wants to offer his friends a last sign that will show them how much he loves them. It will also be a sign of how his kingdom works. So he gets down on his hands and knees and washes their feet.

Peter's reaction suggests how deeply shocked they were – Peter was always the one to blurt out what everyone was thinking, but was too polite to say out loud. Wearing sandals on dusty roads, people of Peter's time often needed their feet washed, especially for a special Passover banquet like this one, but this duty was performed by a servant or a slave – one of the unimportant people on the margins of the Big Picture. By contrast, religious teachers, rabbis, were held in great reverence by their students, who vied with one another to perform little services for the master. So Jesus is exploding the mental categories of his disciples when he serves them like a slave, even though he is in fact, as he tells them after his act, their master. In short, if even the Master serves, everyone who follows him must serve as well; and that is how *his* kingdom works.

John curiously makes no mention in his account of the Last Supper of the Eucharist (which we will consider next week). This is especially strange since he earlier depicts Jesus giving a long discourse on himself as the Bread of Life (John's Gospel, chapter 6). Commentators think that John describes the foot-washing *instead* of the Eucharist, as another way to make the same point. If we are nourished by Jesus, if we take his word deep inside ourselves, we will do the kinds of things he did, and that means "action and more action" (BB, 88), service and more service.

A woman once asked Bill W. how she could thank him for the gift of her recovery; he replied, "Pass it on." Jesus tells his followers the same thing, whether the medium involved is bread to relieve hunger, or water to cleanse and comfort. Feed others as you have been fed; wash others humbly as you have been washed; "pass[ ] on what [you have] learned to others . . . [and] in so doing . . . pay[ ] [your] debt to the [one] who took time to pass it on to [you]" (Dr. Bob's Story, BB, 181).

During this week, let's pray that our commitment to service, renewed during the Second Week, may be strengthened by what we see Jesus doing as his life draws to a close. And let's remember that "[s]ervice, gladly rendered" is one of the "permanent and legitimate satisfactions of right living for which no amount of pomp and circumstance [which Ignatius calls "honors"], no heap of material possessions [Ignatius's "riches"], could possibly be substitutes" (12 X 12, 124).

Second Prelude, to Go: Lord Jesus, help me to freely give what I have freely received.

Meditation 39

The Eucharist

(Lk 22:14-38)

The word "eucharist" means "thanksgiving." At his Last Meal, Jesus gave his friends bread and wine, and told them that by this gesture he was giving himself completely into their hands. He took bread and returned thanks – thanks to God, for everything, his life, his friends, his chance to serve, even his death. And he asked his friends to remember him with such a meal, to remember him thankfully for all that he had given them.

Luke ties this Last Supper and this First Gratitude Potluck to the kingdom. Before Jesus blesses the bread and the cup, he tells his friends that the next time they feast together, it will be in the kingdom of God. (There was a venerable tradition that after the Messiah brought in the kingdom, there would be a great feast that would last forever.) The death Jesus is about to undergo, horrible as it will be, is nonetheless the essential step for bringing about that kingdom, since Jesus' refusal to fight back, his absolute reliance on Abba, will draw for us an unforgettable portrait of the principles of the kingdom. Every time we remember Jesus' gift of bread and wine, we look, not only to the past, when he gave himself for us, but to the future, when we will sit down together with him – and so many other fascinating people – at the Great Meeting.

What Jesus chooses to bless also tells us something about the kingdom, I think. He gives himself as bread, one of the most common foodstuffs there is, available everywhere in the world. Even poor people have bread (or they ought to in a just world). Poverty is no bar to membership in the kingdom – on the contrary, poverty gets you a good table. The gift of wine may startle alcoholics a little, but then Jesus, like A.A., "never . . . show[ed] intolerance or hatred of drinking as an institution" (BB, 103). Indeed, for one of his miracles he provided wine to keep a wedding reception going (Jn 2), and his enemies called him an alcoholic (Mt 11:19). Clearly he realized that "[f]or most normal folks, drinking means conviviality, companionship and . . . joyous intimacy with friends and a feeling that life is good" (BB, 151). And even very poor people can afford wine.

The after-dinner Meeting at the Supper, according to Luke, returns for one last time to the subject of the kingdom. As we have seen, Jesus had spent a lot of time with his disciples, trying to get across to them his unique sense of what the kingdom could be. This meal will be the last chance to teach them in calm words; the events of his Passion will be so tumultuous that they won't get the point of those events for a while. So imagine his dismay when his friends begin to bicker about "who should be regarded as the greatest" in the kingdom (Lk 22:24). They have learned nothing. So, as in John's Gospel, Jesus tells them as plainly as he can that he sees himself as their servant, and that they should expect humbly to imitate him in this regard.

At the same time, in a burst of affection he thanks them for their loyalty to him, and tells them that they will sit on thrones in *his* kingdom, "judging the twelve tribes of Israel" (Lk 22:30). Like a lot of alcoholics, the disciples have trouble keeping two different ideas in their heads at the same time. So instead of trying to combine the notions of service and sitting on thrones – as in Bill W.'s paradoxical concept that "True ambition is the deep desire to live usefully and walk humbly under the grace of God" (12 X 12, 124-5) – they latch on to the throne business and forget the service piece. After all, judging is a lot more fun than serving.

The end of this conversation makes clear that they have, even at this solemn moment, missed the point. Jesus tries to tell them that there are rough times coming very soon, that even Peter, the bold one, is going to falter. It's not going to be like the peaceful ministry they've experienced. Human beings, when they believe they are threatened, have a propensity for violence, and it's going to break out that very night. Jesus uses figurative language, as in his parables, to hint at the disaster that's coming: "[T]he man without a sword must sell his coat and buy one" (Lk 22:36). The disciples, still fixated on thrones and on *their* vision of kingship, take this literally, and try to cheer Jesus up: "No problem! We've got *two* swords!"

At the practical level, this is idiotic; outside of an Arnold Schwarzenegger film, two swords won't do much against all the forces that will be swooping down on Jesus and his followers later that night. But at the spiritual level of Jesus' message, this is downright painful; as Jesus says at the Last Supper in John, "[A]fter I have been with you all this time, you still do not know me?" (Jn 14:9). They still haven't gotten Jesus, and they haven't gotten the kingdom. Violence is the problem, not the solution. With a resigned sigh, Jesus closes this Eucharistic meal, this Gratitude Meeting, with "Enough" (Lk 22:38). He moves on to Gethsemane; what he hasn't been able to get across in words to his friends about his kingdom, he will have to act out for them.

I once heard at a meeting that, at any given moment, a human being can either feel resentment or gratitude.

Let's pray this week that we may always be ready to "trudge the [r]oad" (BB, 164) that leads from resentment to thanksgiving, and especially that we may be grateful whenever we meet people who feed us.

Second Prelude, to Go: Lord Jesus, you have fed me, and I am satisfied; I thank you, and ask that I may feed others in my turn.

Meditation 40

Gethsemane

(Lk 22:39-46)

In the introduction to this book, I told the story of Fr. Eddie Dowling, S.J., and Bill W. Dowling was the Jesuit from St. Louis who sought out Bill in 1940 to tell him that Bill's Twelve Steps and Ignatius' Spiritual Exercises had a lot in common. Afterwards, Dowling was Bill's spiritual director for the rest of the priest's life, twenty years all told. When the Second A.A. International Convention was held in St. Louis in 1955, Bill naturally invited Fr. Dowling to speak.

That speech is reprinted in *A.A. Comes of Age:* it is a strange, moving, poetic, somewhat disjointed attempt to move back and forth between the world of A.A. and the world of Ignatius (as this book does). At one point Dowling offers his own Twelve Steps, not of human beings walking toward God, but of God – in Jesus – coming toward human beings. Like many Jesuits – like me, for instance – Dowling is especially moved by the Incarnation, which in his version is God's First Step, in which God becomes "one of us" (see Meditation 20, above). The Seventh Step is Gethsemane. Dowling describes Jesus' Agony in the Garden like this: "The next step, soul suffering in Gethsemane; that's [God] coming close [to us]. How well the alcoholic knows, and how well [Jesus] knew, humiliation and fear and loneliness and discouragement and futility" (AACA, 258).

People have for centuries found comfort in the thought that even God's Son struggled with God's will the night before he died. Clearly Jesus had "knowledge of [God's] will" for him. Given his very different concept of "the Kingdom," he must have realized that sooner or later the Powers That Be would want to shut him up, whatever that took. And recently he had chosen to proclaim the kingdom on Their turf, in the City, not out in the boondocks of Galilee. This could only spell death for him. What he was praying for in Gethsemane, with "greater intensity," so that "his sweat became like drops [literally, "clots" or "lumps"] of blood falling to the ground" (Lk 22: 44), was "the power to carry that [will of God] out" (Step Eleven).

Remembering this moment in Jesus' life has consoled people, including alcoholics, in "every season of grief or suffering, when the hand of God seemed heavy or even unjust" (12 X 12, 105). This is Jesus modeling what we aspire to in the Third Degree of Humility. When we experience "humiliation and fear and loneliness and discouragement and futility," we know we are not alone; Jesus knew them, too.

Luke links this supreme agony to the Kingdom. Before and after his ordeal, Jesus tells his disciples to pray not to be tempted ("test" in 22: 40 and "trial" in 22: 46 are the same word in Greek). Luke used the same word when he described Jesus' temptations in the desert, at the very beginning of Jesus' ministry: Luke's account of the temptations ends with "When the devil had finished all the *tempting* [same word as "test" and "trial"], he left [Jesus], to await another opportunity" (4: 13) Gethsemane is the other "opportunity"; and the temptation is still the same: "Don't turn your will and your life over to the care of Abba; instead, impose your own will on people and events. The Kingdom is a nice idea, but in the real world, Personal Power is what matters."

This is the "brave philosophy, wherein each [human being] plays God"; it "sounds good in the speaking," which is why human beings have been listening to it since Adam and Eve. Jesus' "election," nevertheless, was to stay true to Abba, and to his own belief that "[t]he philosophy of self-sufficiency is not paying off. Plainly enough, it is a bone-crushing juggernaut whose final achievement is ruin" (12 X 12, 37). And he made this "election" knowing well that it meant that the "juggernaut" would then "crush" him.

In our prayer this week, let us continue in a spirit of gratitude to Jesus, feeling compassion for him who was willing to go so far in feeling compassion for our "humiliation and fear and loneliness and discouragement."

Second Prelude, to Go: Lord Jesus, as you have known my "humiliation and fear and loneliness and discouragement," help me in my turn to know your compassion and your acceptance of God's will.

Meditation 41

Jesus on Trial

(Jn 18:28 to 19:16)

John's version of the Passion of Jesus makes very clear that the "crime" about which Jesus is being grilled by the representative of Roman power is his proclamation of the Kingdom. Nearly everything in this passage refers back to this point: the Roman soldiers, for example, use kingship as the theme of their abuse of Jesus, with a "crown" and a "royal robe," and brutal parodies of court etiquette.

As we have seen in the course of this retreat, the Kingdom is in fact the focus of Jesus' message. The difficulty all along has been that when human beings – any human beings, Roman, Jewish, critics and disciples of Jesus alike, you, me – hear words like "kingdom" and "power," these words hook into all the desires and resentments and fears that trouble us. Again and again, we think, "If only I were king – or queen, or president, or boss – for just *five minutes*, I would 'wrest satisfaction and happiness out of this world' (BB, 61) by making everybody do what I think they should."

Jesus by now has fully grasped that this is the way "the world" understands "power" and "kingship." However, as he points out to Pilate, if he were using these words the way "the world" does, his "subjects would be fighting to save" him (Jn 18:36). No – his mission, his message, his "truth" (Jn 18:37) is that, from Abba's point of view, "kingdom" connotes loving service, not the violent imposition of our wills on other people.

124

In a way, Pilate unconsciously seems to get what Jesus is saying: he lets Jesus be reduced to a pathetic, marginal figure, a mock king, in hopes that people will see that Jesus is harmless. But this is precisely the kind of king that Jesus has chosen to be, united with all the powerless people on the bottom of society, who get beaten up by the people on the next level up. John loves irony, and Jesus' kingdom is ironic, given what we humans think of power. The last irony is that the "powerful" Pilate is utterly powerless to set Jesus free.

The purpose of the Exercises is to prepare us to make, as freely as we can, a life-choice. In our meditation this week, we are close to the climax of the gospel story of Jesus, and the choice is at last completely clear; as the disciples had declared at the Last Supper, "At last [Jesus is] speaking plainly, without talking in veiled language!" (Jn 16: 29). We can choose power; or we can choose, with Jesus, to serve. Power is perhaps the greatest addiction of all, in that of its nature it can never permanently satisfy human beings, as Adam and Eve learned. We eat power, we drink it, and we are hungrier and thirstier than we were before.

Jesus suggests this to Pilate: "You would have no power over me whatever unless it were given you from above" (Jn 19:11). All power is limited; some other people will have as much, or more, than I have, and they will "wish to retaliate, snatching all they can get out of the show" (BB, 61). The other choice – love – has no such limitations: "love freely given surely brings a full return" (12 X 12, 124). But then love has a lot of drawbacks, too: "It may mean the loss of many nights' sleep, great interference with your pleasures, interruptions to your business. It may mean sharing your money and your home, counseling frantic wives and relatives, innumerable trips to police courts, sanitariums, hospitals, jails and asylums" (BB, 97).

In the end, what is our choice to be? Our retreat guides can help us again at this point to strengthen our commitment to exactly what God is asking us to choose. St. John of the Cross, a sixteenth-century Spanish mystic and devoted follower of Jesus, said that "At evening they will examine you in love" (he got the idea from Mt 25:31-46). Let us pray this week that we might have the courage and the gratitude to choose what Jesus chose.

Second Prelude, to Go: Lord Jesus, help me to choose what you chose, that I may bear witness to your power, your love, and your way of life (see Third Step Prayer – BB, 63).

Meditation 42

Jesus' Loved Ones and the Passion

Last week we meditated on people who resisted Jesus' notion of the kingdom, a resistance that brought about his death. It is important that we not think of this as "the wrongs others [have] done" (BB, 67) – a big part of us resists this notion, too, and keeps balking at imitating Jesus by turning our will and our lives over so utterly to God (Third Step). But another part of us wants, however timidly, to follow Jesus on the Way of the Cross. So this week let's consider the followers of Jesus, and their different reactions to his ordeal.

Many of them panicked – understandably. Peter, a "noisy good fellow craving attention and companionship" (12 X 12, 57), really lost control: when Jesus was arrested, Peter drew a sword and attacked one of the arresting officers, a gross violation of the spirit of the kingdom. Clearly Peter was still as horrified by the idea that Jesus would suffer as he had been when Jesus first brought it up. Jesus heals the man Peter wounded, and then he is hauled off to jail. In the face of Jesus' meekness, Peter, the man of action, falls apart. If he can't retaliate, if he can't get physical, he has no idea what to do. And so he does just what Jesus, who knew him so well, predicted he would do; he caves in to the Powers That Be and disclaims Jesus. Just as characteristically, he instantly regrets his denial bitterly; however, enough of Jesus and Abba has rubbed off on Peter that, unlike Judas, he clings to the hope that he can somehow make amends for what he has done.

The other male disciples simply run away. Jesus bargained with the police for this: "It's me you want – let these other guys go." The kingdom is not about retaliation; Jesus wants his to be the only blood that is shed. But after running off, most of the disciples undergo a change of heart, sooner, like Peter, or later. One – "the beloved disciple" – even finds the courage to stand under the cross. How? "We ask [God] to remove our fear and direct our attention to what [God] would have us be. At once, we commence to outgrow fear" (BB, 68).

One person, who had probably never heard of Jesus before, is immediately redeemed by Jesus' suffering: Barabbas. There are a lot of legends about this man. First of all, he may have been more than an ordinary criminal; the words used to describe him in the Gospel may connote that he was a terrorist, a man who used violence to gain political ends. His vision of the kingdom was the polar opposite of Jesus'. Some ancient manuscripts intensify the irony by noting that Barabbas had a first name – Jesus; "Bar-abbas" could mean "Son of Abba." It's as if Barabbas was Jesus of Nazareth's dark twin.

In any case, Barabbas was saved from execution and set free because Jesus was willing to give up his life. Through the centuries many have wondered whether Barabbas took the trouble to learn about his redeemer, even to follow him. Perhaps his experience of a sudden and unexpected "escape from disaster" (BB, 17) changed his "whole attitude and outlook on life" and on the Kingdom (BB, 84).

Finally, a few people took the great risk of staying with Jesus even in this moment of supreme danger. These were the women-disciples, who had followed him all the way from Galilee. John even states that Jesus' own mother was at her son's cross. Perhaps these women were more

receptive to the new kind of reign that Jesus was propos-
ing, a community free of violence, in which the greatest
would serve the least. Or perhaps in a patriarchal society
they knew that, as unimportant people, they had little to
lose in following Jesus to the end. Or perhaps they knew
intuitively that "love is stronger than death" (Song of
Songs 8: 6).

In our prayer this week, we may at different times
identify with some or all of these characters of the Passion. When a loved person dies, those who live on go
through a host of emotions. Whatever our feelings during
the course of this week, let's remember to ask for what
Ignatius suggests: "sorrow with Christ in sorrow, anguish
with Christ in anguish, tears and deep grief because of the
great affliction Christ endures for me" (SE, #203).

Second Prelude, to Go: Lord, help me to grow in compassion, that I may feel what you and all my suffering
sisters and brothers feel.

Meditation 43

Seven Sayings from the Cross

This week I would like to use a traditional form of meditating on the Passion of Jesus, the Seven Words from the Cross (seven sayings, actually; most are more than one word). They were drawn centuries ago from the different Gospels. Sometimes they are used as part of church services on Good Friday; Haydn composed moving musical evocations of each of them. I think they can help us to realize Ignatius' goal for us this week, which is to feel "sorrow with Christ in sorrow" (SE, #203).

First Saying: "Father, forgive them; they do not know what they are doing" (Lk 23:34).

Some ancient manuscripts do not have this verse; but it sounds very much like the Jesus we have come to know in this retreat, who came to speak "the truth" about the Kingdom. The Kingdom is about forgiveness and reconciliation, not retaliation. Jesus asks Abba to forgive Jesus' human brothers and sisters; Jesus knows profoundly now how confused we are. As we try to follow Jesus every step of his way, we might renew our commitment to the process of forgiveness provided by the Steps, and especially by Step Five: "Our moral inventory had persuaded us that all-round forgiveness was desirable, but it was only when we resolutely tackled Step Five that we inwardly *knew* we'd be able to receive forgiveness and give it, too" (12 X 12, 58; italics Bill's).

Second Saying: To one of the criminals dying alongside Jesus: "I assure you: this day you will be with me in paradise" (Lk 23:43).

As I note when I study this passage in my next book (see Year C, Palm Sunday and Feast of Christ the King), this saying tells us a lot about the kingdom of Jesus. His kingdom, like "the Realm of Spirit," "is broad, roomy, all inclusive; never exclusive or forbidding to those who earnestly seek." Last-minute conversions are perfectly acceptable. The only requirement for membership is "a willingness to believe" (BB, 46). In fact, Jesus from the Beatitudes on felt that people like this criminal were better prospects for the kingdom, because they are "as open-minded to conviction and as willing to listen as the dying can be" (12 X 12, 24). The kingdom of Jesus is ironic: "*today*" the doomed criminal will be in paradise. Like the "eleventh-hour" workers in one of Jesus' parables (Mt 20:1-16), he cuts into the line into heaven way ahead of the "virtuous." Out of this criminal's "season of grief" on his cross will come "the conviction . . . that God does 'move in a mysterious way [God's] wonders to perform'" (12 X 12, 105).

Third Saying: To his mother, about "the beloved disciple": "Woman, there is your son." To the disciple, about his mother: "There is your mother" (Jn 19:26, 27).

One of the greatest statues ever carved is Michelangelo's *Pieta*; it shows Mary holding her dead son, Jesus, in her arms. Every parent who has lost a child, particularly to violence or war, can empathize with Mary. Is there any possible response to grief this profound? Jesus offers one in this saying: if we are disciples of his, we will fashion from our suffering a way to sustain others, to build up the kingdom. Bill W. put it this way: "Can we transform . . .

calamities into assets, sources of growth and comfort to ourselves and those about us? Well, we surely have a chance . . . if we are willing to receive that grace of God which can sustain and strengthen us in any catastrophe" (12 X 12, 112). St. Paul makes the same point: "[God] comforts us in all our afflictions and thus enables us to comfort those who are in trouble, with the same consolation we have received from [God]" (2 Cor 1:4).

Fourth Saying: *"'Eli, Eli, lema sabachtani?,'* that is, 'My God, my God, why have you forsaken me?' " (Mt 27:46).

Jesus is quoting Psalm 22 here; Matthew gives the Aramaic words for it, in part because these are Jesus' solemn last words before his death in Matthew, in part because Matthew often stresses how Jesus brings to fulfillment everything in the Hebrew Scriptures. So, like John's "Now it is finished" (see Sixth Saying, below), this quotation is a statement of accomplishment. But, like the Agony in Gethsemane, these words have also been a source of consolation for many over the centuries who felt abandoned by God, "cut off from God's help and direction" (12 X 12, 105). Even Jesus, with his deep trust in Abba, struggled with this last temptation. However, these desolate words are only the beginning of Psalm 22; towards the end of it, the psalmist says, "God has listened to the cry for help of the poor man. . . . to God, ruler of the nations, belongs kingly power" (Ps 22:24, 27). Jesus is thinking of Abba, the ruler who favors the poor. "We know," as Jesus knew, "that God lovingly watches over us. We know that when we turn to [God], all will be well with us, here and hereafter" (12 X 12, 105).

Fifth Saying: "I am thirsty" (Jn 19:28).

Like Matthew, John depicts the dying Jesus alluding to Psalm 22 "to fulfill the Scripture." The psalm is much more vivid than this simple phrase (one word in Greek): "My throat is dried up like baked clay, my tongue cleaves to my jaws; to the dust of death you have brought me down" (Ps 22:16). John, with his eye for theological symbolism, wants us to recall that Jesus is undergoing this thirst to release the "rivers of living waters" he had promised earlier (Jn 7:37). But this saying should also touch us at the ordinary, human level: one of the horrible things about death by crucifixion, naked in the blazing sun of Palestine, would be the thirst. Those of us who are alcoholics also know something of a thirst that nothing could satisfy, until we found – or were found by – a Power that grew from "a trickle" to "a river" (12 X 12, 109). John may also want to remind us of Jesus' encounter with a Samaritan woman (Jn 4), which began with Jesus asking her for a drink of water; as St. Augustine pointed out, Jesus was actually thirsting for her faith, he was thirsting to carry the message of the kingdom. Let's pray that his thirst to serve may be in us as well.

Sixth Saying: "Now it is finished" (Jn 19:30)

This is Jesus' last saying before his death in John. The Greek word does not connote failure or despair; instead it means, "It is completely accomplished" or "achieved." What God wanted done has been done: the message has been carried. In Jesus' death anyone who wants to can see who Abba is – the loving father of the story of the Prodigal Son. Abba responds to our human craziness, our resentment and fear, not with rage and brutality – those are *our* specialties – but with forgiveness. The final temptation has been successfully resisted; Jesus has completely carried out the will of Abba. Now, "[h]aving . . . considered" his life, having taken "due note of things well done, and having searched [his] heart with neither fear nor favor, [he] . . . truly thank[s] God for the blessings [he has] received and sleep[s] in good conscience" (12 X 12, 95).

Seventh Saying: "Father, into your hands I commend my spirit" (Lk 23:46).

Luke gives these as Jesus' last words before his death. It's a peaceful close; Luke likes to portray Jesus at prayer, and these words are between Jesus and Abba. Jesus is quoting another psalm here: "You will free me from the snare they set for me, for you are my refuge. Into your hands I commend my spirit; you will redeem me, O Lord, O faithful God" (Ps 31:4-5). The very last thing he does is turn his will and his life over to the care of God as he understands God (Third Step). What was the result for him? The same as for any other human being who takes this Step: he felt, even at this last moment, "new power flow in," he enjoyed "peace of mind," he became "conscious of [God's] presence." He was somehow, even while dying, "reborn" (BB, 63). Let us practice this Step every day of our lives.

Second Prelude, to Go: Dear God, may I do Thy will always (see the Third Step Prayer – BB, 63).

Meditation 44

Summary Reflections on the Passion

In last week's meditation on the last words of Jesus, following an ancient devotional practice we skipped around in the Gospels. This week I want to take up the Gospel accounts of Jesus' death in a different way, by studying the Gospels in the order in which they were composed. My aim is to give a sense of the deepening understanding by the Christian community of the meaning of his death over the years that followed it.

Mark's was the first Gospel. It is the most vivid and the most immediate. Mark includes some raw facts that the later evangelists soften in some embarrassment, for example, that Jesus' family thought he was crazy to preach his kind of kingdom, or that his disciples were deeply baffled by his message through virtually all the time he spent with them. So Mark's account of Jesus' death is harsh and unsparing; note that Jesus' only "word" from the cross in Mark is the anguished "My God, my God, why have you forsaken me?" In Mark the two criminals crucified with Jesus (in Mark they are "insurgents," believers in a violent kingdom) simply "taunt" him, as do the crowds.

Nonetheless, one person grasps the meaning of what's happening – of all people, a Gentile, the Roman centurion, who is standing guard over the crucified ones. He says, "Clearly this man was the Son of God!" (Mk 15:39). This is the theme of Mark's Gospel, stated in the first verse of his first chapter. For people with faith, this truth is visible even in the terrible circumstances of Jesus'

135

death, *if* you buy into Jesus' concept of the Kingdom as
loving service.

The evangelists who followed Mark draw out this
theme more explicitly. In Matthew and Luke, written
probably about the same time, some decades after Mark,
the tone is softer: Pilate's wife urges him not to "interfere
in the case of that holy man" (Mt 27:19); Luke, as we saw
last week, includes Jesus' prayer for forgiveness for his
executioners, as well as the colloquy with the repentant
criminal, and Jesus' commending of his spirit to Abba.
Mark sees the crucifixion in large part as something terrible that nevertheless must happen if the kingdom is to
come later; Matthew and Luke see little signs that the
kingdom is in fact beginning even now, during the Passion – "this day you will be with me in paradise."

John, probably the last to write, characteristically
builds on the earlier Gospels so he can go more deeply
into the meaning of the events of Jesus' life, and this is
true of the Passion as well. In John, the kingdom begins
to dawn at the moment when Judas goes out from the
Last Supper to set events in motion: Jesus immediately
says, "Now is the Son of Man glorified and God is glorified
in him" (Jn 13:31). John sees the events of the Passion as
at once terrible and glorious, since they are such a clear
"sign" (an important word in John) of the kingdom, of
who God is. John portrays Pilate as much taken with Jesus;
John omits mention of the jeering crowds. In this Gospel,
Jesus makes arrangements for the care of his loved ones;
and he rounds off his life with the pronouncement that
God's will has been fully achieved.

This growing sense of Jesus' death as freely embraced
to show forth God's love, rather than as a miserable catastrophe bravely endured, is clear particularly at the very
moment of Jesus' death. Mark and Luke both say that Je-

sus "expired," literally, "breathed out." Matthew begins to
see more in this than just a last breath: he rewords Mark
to say that Jesus "gave up his spirit" (Mt 27:50; "spirit" and
"breath" are the same word in Greek). Theologically, John
puts the finishing touch on this by saying that Jesus "deliv-
ered over his spirit"; the phrase could also be translated,
"he handed over the Spirit" (Jn 19:30).

John's phrasing makes two important points: first, as
Jesus had insisted, he was giving up his life *willingly* – no
one was taking it from him (Jn 10:18). Second, Jesus is
giving us *his* Spirit, as he had promised the night before, at
the Last Supper; since the glory, and the kingdom, have
already begun with the events of his Passion, his Spirit of
loving service is now available to all who would follow him.

As we conclude the Third Week, let us keep John's
thought in mind: we have been witnessing more than just
another tragic instance of how inhumanly human beings
can treat one of their own. In Jesus' willingness to do
God's will, even at this price, is the beginning of glory, of
hope that all human beings can be restored to sanity
(Step Two). St. Irenaeus, an early Christian writer, observed that "The glory of God is a human being fully
alive." With the irony that characterizes the kingdom of
Jesus, we can believe that never was Jesus so gloriously
alive as at the moment of his death, when he gave himself
fully into God's hands – and ours.

Second Prelude, to Go: Lord Jesus, you have put your
life in my hands; grant that I may show my gratitude to
you by passing it on.

✢

Fourth Week

─────────────

"Being all powerful, [God] provided what we
needed, if we kept close to [God] and performed
[God's] work well. Established on such a footing
we became less and less interested in ourselves. . . .
More and more we became interested in seeing
what we could contribute to life. As we felt new
power flow in, as we enjoyed peace of mind, as
we discovered we could face life successfully, as
we became conscious of [God's] presence, we began to lose our fear of today, tomorrow or the
hereafter. We were reborn" (BB, 63).

Our retreat guides have now pointed us to the Fourth
Week. During this Week, Ignatius wants us to consider
two closely related topics: rebirth, and specifically the resurrection of Jesus, and love. As this quotation from the
Big Book suggests, love and service are our best clues to
what becomes of us "today, tomorrow, or [in] the hereafter." God is "all powerful," our source of "new power"; if
God has the power to give us relief from "a seemingly
hopeless state of mind and body" (BB, xiii), then it makes
sense to go on to Step Three, as Jesus did throughout his
life, and put our lives in God's powerful and loving hands.
The St. Francis Prayer puts it this way: "Lord, grant that I
may seek rather to comfort than to be comforted – to understand, than to be understood – to love, than to be
loved. For it is by self-forgetting that one finds. It is by

forgiving that one is forgiven. It is by dying that one awakens to Eternal Life" (12 X 12, 99). If we can trust God with our lives, we can trust God with our deaths and with whatever lies after them.

We may have made, or renewed, some of our life-choices during the Second Week. We renewed our commitment to service, to discipleship. Then, during the Third Week, we caught a glimpse of the cost of that discipleship, as Dietrich Bonhoeffer did in a Nazi prison. Now, in the Fourth Week, we begin to sense the ultimate results of choosing to suffer with Jesus: "we begin to see truth, justice, and love as the real and eternal things in life. . . . We know that when we turn to [God], all will be well with us, here and hereafter" (12 X 12, 105).

This Week, as we contemplate Christ's awakening early on Easter Sunday, Ignatius invites us to focus on three aspects of the resurrection experience. First, he invokes the old story that Jesus, like a Joseph Campbell hero, traveled through the underworld during the time of his death: "there he sets free [literally, "pulls out"] the souls of the just" (SE, #219). Jesus' death and resurrection occurred, according to the Gospels, around the time of Passover, the commemoration of the Exodus; and liberation, "a new freedom" (BB, 83), was in the air. Jesus is the new Moses, the new Liberator, setting us free from "strife/And old debate/And hate" (Robert Herrick, "To Keep a True Lent").

Second, Ignatius naturally believes that the predominating emotion this Week will be joy: we should "ask for the grace to be glad and rejoice intensely because of the great joy and the glory of Christ the Lord" (SE, #221). Recall that in John's account, the glory of Christ – which is the glory of God (see Jn 17) – begins with Jesus' loving farewell at the Last Supper and continues through the crucifixion; so much glory leads inevitably to the glory of the resurrection. Having walked through life and death with Jesus in the retreat so far, we now walk on to new life; and seeing what God has done for Jesus makes us "happy, joyous, and free" (BB, 133).

Finally, Ignatius bids us to consider Jesus in "the office of consoler that Christ our Lord exercises, and compare it with the way in which friends are wont to [i.e., usually] console one another" (SE, #224). "Office" is used here in an older sense; it means "type of service." In other words, Jesus, having had a spiritual awakening, carries the message to his friends, and comforts them for their loss of him – even comforts them for the guilt they feel about not having been there for him in his hour of need (see Meditation 48, below). There is no limit to the compassion that Jesus, as child of Abba, feels for his all-too-human sisters and brothers. Now he knows from his own experience what the fear of death is like, and how it drives human beings to "liv[e] upon a basis of unsatisfied demands" (12 X 12, 76). But it doesn't have to be this way, which is why his first word to his gathered friends after his resurrection is "Peace" (Jn 20:19, 21).

During this Week, let us ask God for a deepening sense of the gifts the risen Christ brings us, and above all "a new freedom and a new happiness" (BB, 83).

Meditation 45

The Garden

(Jn 20:1-18)

"We've got to get ourselves back to the garden."
— Joni Mitchell

At the end of his account of the Passion, John noted that Jesus' tomb was in a garden (Jn 19:41). The events of this section of John's next chapter take place in this garden. Mary Magdalene even mistakes Jesus for the gardener when she first encounters him (Jn 20:15).

As I have mentioned before, John loves irony and symbolism, and both are at work in this passage. Ironically, Jesus actually is a kind of gardener — he has brought the whole human race, all the children of Adam and Eve, back into the Garden. He did this by reversing the choice of Adam and Eve; where they "balked" (BB, 58) at the Third Step, he had enough trust in Abba to take it, and to stick to it even when it meant "death, death on a cross" (Phil 2: 8). St. Paul goes on to draw the conclusion: "Because of this [Jesus' acceptance of God's will], God highly exalted [Christ]" by raising him to new life.

The Gospels all agree that the first people to see the reborn Jesus in the Garden were the last people to see him alive — the women, like Mary Magdalene, who had followed him throughout his ministry. In Matthew, Mark, and Luke they see Jesus because they are performing the humblest of services: they have come to the tomb to give him a proper burial. If we want to see new life, we need to follow the women's lead, and stay close to those who suffer, at times even when it seems hopeless.

It seems as though the meeting in the Garden with Mary Magdalene that John describes was a spontaneous, "unplanned" gesture of consolation on Jesus' part; perhaps he didn't want her to have to continue weeping when it was in fact a time to rejoice. Anyway, he apologizes for having to rush off; he hasn't yet gone home to Abba, and he can barely wait (in John's version; Luke handles this differently). Only after that visit will he come to all the disciples, including Peter and "the beloved disciple," for his first "official" visit "on the evening of that first day of the week" (20:19). But for now "Morning has broken/Like the first morning [of the Creation]," in the Garden. And Jesus "does not make too hard terms with those who seek him" (BB, 46); so Mary Magdalene gets this special, flying visit.

Ignatius postulates another special visit by the risen Jesus to a woman, but not in a garden. The retreatant is invited to imagine Jesus returning to his mother, Mary. By the way, Ignatius testily observes that anyone who would object that this isn't in the Bible would have to be pretty stupid – what kind of consoler would Jesus be if he didn't console his own mother (SE, #299)?

So this is how the Kingdom begins – sometimes with individuals, sometimes with small groups (women only), sometimes with larger groups. "Little clusters of twos and threes and fives of us have sprung up in other communities. . . . Thus we grow" (BB, 162). Tended by the Gardener, our "roots [can] grasp[ ] a new soil" (BB, 12). When we meet the risen Jesus, we find "that a new power, peace, happiness and sense of direction flow[ ] into [us]" (BB, 50). During our prayer this week, let's pray that our own experience of recovery may make us joyous – and grateful.

Second Prelude, to Go: Lord Jesus, Risen Friend, give me the joy of serving you by consoling those you love.

Meditation 46

The Road to Emmaus

(Lk 24:13-35)

I study this beloved story at length in my next book (Third Sunday of Easter, Year A; Easter, Year C). Some of what I say there would fit well in the context of the Exercises.

To begin with, note that these two disciples have made an "election" at a very bad time (something like what Ignatius calls "desolation" – see Appendix A, on discernment): they have decided to give up on following Jesus when they are distraught over his death, having no clue as to what that death might mean. They have completely failed to get Jesus' central point, about the Kingdom. They "were hoping that he was the one who would set Israel free" (Lk 24:21). But, like practically all the male disciples, they had assumed that Jesus would liberate his people by military force, despite all Jesus kept saying to the contrary. Given this misconception, his dreadful death could only mean the whole thing had been a big mistake.

As the risen Jesus points out, however, it was *their* mistake: "What little sense you have!" (24:25). He spells out for them the concept that we have spent this whole retreat trying to embrace, heart and mind: "the Messiah [the anointed King] [had] to undergo all this so as to enter into his glory" (24:26). We will have to go down the same road if we want to follow him to the end.

Their time with this Stranger leaves them with burning hearts – they have had a spiritual awakening. And as a result of this, they instantly decide to carry the message. Even though they're back home in Emmaus, where they could pick up the pieces of their old lives, even though it's dark, a bad time for foot-travellers, they travel back to Jerusalem, where their leader was recently brutally killed, to tell their story. They "come in the door shouting the good news" (12 X 12, 83): "Then they recounted what had happened on the road and how they had come to know [Jesus] in the breaking of the bread" (24:35).

This short version of their story emphasizes two connected points. "[It] . . . happened on the road" reminds us that the spiritual life, and in particular the following of Jesus, are journeys that involve taking many steps. We will meet Jesus, we will find new life, among the strangers we encounter on "the Road of Happy Destiny" (BB, 164).

Which leads to a second point: how will we know it's Jesus? The same way these two disciples did: "in the breaking of the bread." Wherever people are being fed, with actual bread or the bread that is wisdom, that is the Word of God, there you will meet Jesus. Jesus is wherever his story is told and his message of the kingdom is carried to others. Having begun this retreat with the First Step, as we draw to its close we have come around to the Twelfth.

Second Prelude, to Go: Lord Jesus, Risen Friend, help me to feed others as you have fed and nourished me.

Meditation 47

Jesus Returns to His Home Group

(Lk 24:36-49)

This week's Gospel passage comes immediately after last week's. The two disciples from Emmaus, whom Jesus 12th-Stepped back from their "slip," have re-merged with the rest of the group. We do not hear about them again. The only requirement for membership in the Kingdom is a desire to share bread, as Jesus did with them; and the two lost-and-found disciples have that desire, that willingness, once again. No questions asked.

The Gospel writers make clear that, for a lot of disciples, faith in the risen Jesus was very much a matter of *coming* to believe, as it was for the Guys from Emmaus. Some at first thought they were seeing a ghost; some "were still incredulous [literally, "didn't have faith"] for sheer joy and wonder" (Lk 24:41; see Mt 28:17, where "some doubted" the risen Jesus).

"To those of us who have hitherto known only excitement, depression, or anxiety – in other words, to all of us" (12 X 12, 74) – such incredible good news can be very hard to believe at first. When we finally began to experience recovery – when we finally "learn[ed] the full meaning of 'Love thy neighbor as thyself'" (BB, 153) – it may have seemed like a waking dream. We may have felt like ghosts ourselves, back from the dead, revisiting our old haunts, but with this difference: like Jesus, we were real, not ghosts, and we could prove it by sharing food with other people.

146

After Jesus eats with his home-group again, he goes over the same points he made to the two deserters on the way to Emmaus. As human beings, we want to know what suffering means, and so he tells his friends that his own suffering and resurrection had to happen for the kingdom to begin. It turns out that this is what "Messiah" really meant in the sacred writings, all along. At the Last Supper, he had promised that the next time he ate, it would be "in the kingdom of God" (Lk 22:16); he's eating now, honey and fish, so the kingdom has begun, his kind of kingdom, a kingdom of peace. And that is what they are to preach "to all nations" (Lk 24:47).

What do they need if they are finally going to believe in Jesus' vision of the reign of God? One "essential" is "open mindedness" (see BB, 570, on "Spiritual Experience"). So Jesus "open[s] their minds" (Lk 24:45) so they can begin to understand and believe in him and his kingdom. But one more thing is needed: they suffer from "lack of power" (BB, 45), so Jesus tells them to wait for that power, which is "the promise of the Father" (24:49). He means the Spirit, *his* Spirit, the power that has enabled him to live and die and live anew with trust in God and love of others. Luke ends his Gospel before the sending of the Spirit; that's a whole other story, and Luke covers it in his sequel to the Gospel, the Acts of the Apostles.

We are drawing near the end of this retreat. During this week, let us ask that we might receive God's "promise," the powerful, loving Spirit of Jesus, so that we might play our part in the building of the City of God.

Second Prelude, to Go: Dear God, send down on me the Spirit of Jesus, the greatest of your Promises.

Meditation 48

The Risen Jesus at the Sea of Galilee

(Jn 21)

As I recommended in my next book (Third Sunday of Easter, Year C), it's useful in studying this Gospel selection to imagine that it recounts the first time Jesus appeared to these disciples after the resurrection. There were several versions of Jesus' appearances that circulated in the infant Christian community: one set of stories takes place in Jerusalem (like the readings from Luke and John on which we have meditated for the last three weeks), while others take place in Galilee, like this "appendix" to John's Gospel, or like the end of Matthew's Gospel. After all, Jesus' ministry originally began in Galilee, so he and his friends might well have wanted to return to their roots.

The author of this appendix to the Gospel of John tries to square it with the other Gospels (verse 14). Nevertheless, what happens in this story will make more sense if we take it as a *first* meeting of the risen Jesus and his friends. If we take it this way, it may remind us of the story of the Emmaus disciples. Like them, Simon Peter and his friends have given up and gone home, back to their day jobs as fishermen, back to the nets and the boat they had left when Jesus first called them to be disciples. Like the Emmaus folks, these fishermen at first do not recognize Jesus. As with them (and with the Jerusalem Group last week), it is a meal that finally identifies Jesus

148

to them – a meal of bread and fish, both important signs of the presence of Jesus.

In addition, the effect of Jesus' appearance is the same here as it is in the Emmaus story: the ex-disciples do a turn-around (which in Latin is *conversio*) and become disciples again. In the case of John 21, the focus is particularly on the chief disciple, Simon Peter. The scene recalls his original summons to discipleship (see Meditation 26, above), which in Luke takes place beside the Sea of Galilee and involves a remarkable catch of fish. In that first scene, back when the world was younger, Peter had had misgivings about answering Jesus' call because Peter was in the First Week and on the First Step, deeply aware of his failings. This time around, he is feeling even worse, because now he has denied Jesus three times. On top of that, he has quit and gone home, and invited other disciples to do the same, which surely doesn't look very loyal. So what will Jesus do to this pygmy of faith, once so boastful?

This is not a case of "no questions asked";⌈for healing to occur, some things need to be said out loud.⌋ Peter's recovery of his discipleship, his repairing this "twisted" and "broken relationship" (12 X 12, 78), depends on his "capacity to be honest" (BB, 58). But the questions Jesus asks are not what we might have asked – for instance, "Why did you deny me?" or "Why are you back fishing in Galilee, where I first called you?" Or even worse, "Why didn't you lay down your life for me when push came to shove, like you swore you would just a few hours before?" Instead, the question is gentler, but at the same time maybe even more harrowing: "Do you love me?"

In Greek Jesus' first question uses the word for "unselfish, generous love," which perhaps puts Peter on the hot seat even more; when he first replies that he "loves" Jesus, he humbly substitutes a milder word, something like

"I'm fond of you." Peter is not going to indulge in over-statement this time. Jesus lowers the stakes with each question, from "unselfishly love me *more than the others*" (1) to "unselfishly love me" (2) to "are fond of me" (3) – on the third question he uses Peter's word. Peter sticks to his humbler word all through, and only adds to his third reply that Jesus knows him – only too well? – and so Jesus must know that Peter "is fond of you." Peter's three denials are amended by three modest avowals.

The point of all this is not primarily to make Peter feel better. Like all the Steps, this "Ninth Step" is meant to help Peter (and others who work the Steps) give better service, which is why Jesus tells him three times to feed people as Jesus feeds them.

The punchline of this episode comes in verse 19: Jesus renews Peter's original call to discipleship with the words "Follow me." We have come to understand in this retreat that following Jesus, discipleship, means doing God's will, which may well not be our will at all. Nevertheless, even by our deaths, if we accept them as God's will, we "glorify God" (21:18), as Jesus did by freely accepting his death, and as Peter will, some day down the road.

This retreat is almost over. But as we begin to think about resuming our lives, let's continue to ask God to renew our call to discipleship by helping us to share in the joy, and the consoling service, of the risen Jesus.

Second Prelude, to Go: Dear God, help me to find joy in your will for me, even when it takes me where I don't want to go.

Meditation 49

Getting the Love of God (Part I)

With our retreat guides, we are sensing that we are coming to the end of this spiritual journey. At the conclusion of the Spiritual Exercises, Ignatius sums up everything he has been trying to say about God all through: God as he understands God is "loving," as in Tradition Two. So the last Exercise is the Contemplation to Attain the Love of God. And love is the message that retreatants will carry with them as they resume "all normal activities" (BB, 131); this is the principle above all principles that retreatants will try to practice in all their affairs.

Ignatius offers a few preliminary remarks about this Contemplation, and I have a few of my own. Me first. I want to mention that "Attain" here translates *alcanzar*. A Spanish dictionary informs me that it means "get hold of," and derives from the word for "talon" or "claw" – what hawks use to clutch what they desire. If this is so, then an English translation could be "Contemplation to 'Get' the Love of God," using "get" in the slang sense of "grasp," as in the phrase, "Oh, I get it now."

Above all, "attain" does *not* mean "earn," or "work up to." As is clear from the body of the Contemplation, Ignatius agrees with most spiritually wise people that the love of God is a given; it does not have to be earned, it can't be earned, because we have it from the get-go. This squares with an important principle in the spiritual life: it is easier to make good choices, or to accept painful events, out of gratitude than it is out of duty. I can do

151

more things if I know I have been loved than if I think that I ought to do them.

Ignatius' preliminary remarks to the Contemplation are mostly common sense, but they may still come as news to people whose relationships tend to become addictive and compulsive. "The first is that love ought to manifest itself in deeds rather than in words" (SE, #230). In active addiction, we tend to misuse the words "love me"; what we really mean is "help me stay addicted." So one of the things we recover in recovery is an understanding of the real meaning of love, much as Peter did in last week's meditation. To paraphrase Forrest Gump, Love is as love does.

Ignatius's second preliminary point is "that love consists in a mutual sharing of goods . . . one [lover] always gives to the other" (SE, #231). Again, this underscores for addicts the impossibility of loving and practicing an addiction simultaneously; if you must have all you can lay hands on of something or someone, you can't possibly share it with someone else, so you can't really love. In this preliminary point Ignatius is also setting up his Contemplation, since the focus there will be on a "loving God" as the Great Giver, as the One Who Shares Gifts with all creatures.

Finally, Ignatius, as he often does, tells us what to ask for in our prayer (Second Prelude). This time we are "to ask for an intimate knowledge of the many blessings received, that filled with gratitude for all, I may in all things love and serve the Divine Majesty" (SE, #233). "Intimate knowledge" and "filled with gratitude" both connote a deep-down, mind-and-heart realization of God's gifts to us. Our life-choices, whatever they may be, should involve our most grateful, and most skillful, use of those gifts.

There are four points in the Contemplation proper. I want to study the first two this week, and save the last two until next week. There is some overlap between the points, but don't worry about that – the point is to grow in gratitude, not to put all of God's gifts into the "right" categories.

In the First Point, Ignatius suggests that we "recall to mind the blessings of creation and redemption, and the special favors [we] have received." God made us who we are, with a set of gifts exquisitely fitted to the service only we, out of all the human beings who are now or who have ever been, can give. And just when we thought that all those gifts would probably be thrown away because of our unconquerable attachments, God led us to freedom. In fact, we have seen "how our experience" – our experience of darkness and disaster – "can benefit others" (BB, 84).

Ignatius goes on: "I will ponder with great affection how much God our Lord has done for me, and how much [God] has given me of what [God] possesses" – lovers share all they have – "and finally, how much, as far as [God] can, the same Lord desires to give Himself [or Herself] to me." This leads, with the inevitable logic of love, to a desire on our part to give ourselves in return. We are back to the Colloquy of the First Week, in which we asked what we ought to do for Christ, but with two differences: now, after the whole retreat, we know and love Christ better than we did at the start. And instead of asking what we *ought* to do, we are considering what we will do "with great affection" in return for so much love.

At this moment, and after each of the Four Points of the Contemplation, Ignatius suggests we say a prayer that captures this rhythm of gift-exchange between God and us. This is the much-beloved "*Suscipe*" (from the first word of the prayer in Latin, "Take"). I have had the chutzpah to combine this prayer with the Eleventh Step, and will offer the result in three segments. When we have finished with this Contemplation next week, I will offer my prayer – which I have named "The Giving Prayer" – fully assembled. Here is the first part of it:

> *Take me, O God, and make use of me. Make use of*
> *   all of me –*
> *my freedom, to stop compulsively misusing myself*
> *   or other creatures;*
> *my memory, to recall events and people fondly*
> *   and gratefully;*
> *my understanding, to see the world and people as*
> *   affectionately and compassionately as you do;*
> *my will, to choose wisely and lovingly.*

(12-Steppers may be reminded here of the Third Step Prayer [BB, 63].)

Ignatius, who was educated in late-medieval theology, naturally thought in terms of "faculties of the soul" like "memory," "understanding," and "will," but recovering people can use healing in all these "faculties," too, however they conceive of the human mind and heart. In any case, coming to use our wills "rightly" is "the purpose of A.A.'s Twelve Steps" (12 X 12, 40); and attaining "freedom" is the goal of both the Twelve Steps and the Spiritual Exercises.

In the Second Point of the Contemplation, Ignatius shifts the kaleidoscope slightly: having thought about God's direct gifts to me, I now consider God's indirect gifts. I "reflect how God dwells in creatures: in the elements [rocks and rivers, for instance] . . . in the plants . . . in the animals . . . in human beings" (SE, #235). This Point evokes a central feature of Ignatius' spirituality: since God makes a home in all things, God can be found in all things. Nothing in creation is untouched by God, although it may take some looking in the case of certain creatures. Ignatius goes on to bring this back to ourselves; since we are creatures, too, God is at home in us (a favorite notion of the Gospel of John). God makes us God's "temple" (a favorite notion of St. Paul's).

Our response to this Second Point will be, once again, to say Ignatius' prayer. Here is the second part of my version of it:

> *You gave me all these, and so much more . . . .*
> *You have given me everyone I know or will ever know,*
> *everything I have or am,*
> *even what I don't understand or don't really want –*
> *TODAY.*

We might recall the Seventh Step prayer at this point (BB, 76). God removes those character defects of mine that "stand in the way of my usefulness to [God] and my fellows" – *not*, alas, the ones that make me cringe.

Each of us will have a different gratitude list, because each of us has a unique set of gifts, carefully crafted so we can "be of maximum helpfulness to others" (BB, 102). During this week we may want to get this list in writing, to make our "great affection" for God more concrete.

Second Prelude, to Go: [For this week, please use the parts of The Giving Prayer given in this week's meditation.]

Meditation 50

Getting the Love of God (Part II)

This week we will continue with the Contemplation to "Get" the Love of God. You may well find that last week's concepts and feelings spill over into this week, and that's fine, since this week's reflections will be briefer.

Ignatius' Third Point uses a different metaphor to get across the idea of the Second Point. We were grateful last week that God makes a home in creatures, including ourselves; in the Third Point, we "consider how God works and labors for [us] in all creatures upon the face of the earth. . . . Thus, in the heavens, the elements, the plants, the fruits, the cattle, etc., God gives being, conserves them, confers life and sensation, etc." (SE, #236).

God works; God doesn't just sit there, letting things take their course, with an occasional wistful sigh about how messy creation is getting to be. The implication for us is obvious: "There is action and more action" (BB, 88) — there is work and more work for *us* to do, building the kingdom, building the City of God. But we will never have to work alone.

The last Point of the Contemplation steps back and puts together everything cited so far into one grand vision. In fact, this Point draws on a powerful mystical experience Ignatius had early in his conversion. This experience shaped for the rest of his life the way he saw God in the world. In this Fourth Point we "consider all blessings and gifts as descending from above. Thus, my limited power comes from the supreme and infinite power above, and so, too, justice, goodness, mercy, etc., descend from above as the rays of light descend from the sun, and as the waters flow from their fountains" (SE, #237). Gifts go in an endless cycle, from "infinite God" to "our finite selves" (BB, 68), and, implicitly, back from us, through service to our fellow creatures, to God. This cycle of gratitude is like "the sunlight of the Spirit" (BB, 66); it has "the certainty and majesty of a great tide at flood" (BB, 56).

Our response to both these Points, once again, will be to say Ignatius' Prayer. Here is the final portion of my version:

> *I give it all to you to use as seems good to you.*
>
> *I believe that you will see to it that all of me is used well.*
>
> *And so I ask only for knowledge of your will for me,*
> *for your will is wholly loving;*
>
> *And I ask for the grace and the power to carry out your will.*
>
> *And that's enough.*

Here, at the end of the Giving Prayer, I have tried to fuse two of the greatest gifts God has given me: Jesuit spirituality, the source of Ignatius' *Suscipe*; and the Twelve Steps, including Step Eleven, on which I am drawing in this portion of my Prayer. One last word: "enough," as I often say, is not a word I use lightly or easily. It was a large part of my alcoholism always to worry that there wouldn't be enough of what I was attached to. I suspect most other addicted people have just as much trouble with the idea of having enough, or being enough. Bill W. thought so: "We [alcoholics] eat, drink, and grab for more of everything than we need, fearing we shall never have enough." "Never was there enough of what we thought we wanted" (12 X 12, 49, 71).

What is finally enough – *who* is finally enough – is God, who is even more than "a loving God": as John succinctly puts it in his First Letter, God *is* love. As recovering people, we can finally accept the words that St. Paul in prayer heard from Jesus: "My grace is enough for you, for in weakness power reaches perfection" (2 Cor 12:9).

Here, fully assembled, is The Giving Prayer:

The Giving Prayer

Take me, O God, and make use of me. Make use of all of me –

my freedom, to stop compulsively misusing myself or other creatures;

my memory, to recall events and people fondly and gratefully;

my understanding, to see the world and people as affectionately and compassionately as you do;

my will, to choose wisely and lovingly.

You gave me all these, and so much more . . . .

You have given me everyone I know or will ever know, everything I have or am, even what I don't understand or don't really want – TODAY.

I give it all to you to use as seems good to you.

I believe that you will see to it that all of me is used well.

And so I ask only for knowledge of your will for me, for your will is wholly loving;

And I ask for the grace and the power to carry out your will.

And that's enough.

Second Prelude, to Go: [For this week, please use this complete version of The Giving Prayer.]

Meditation 51

Preparing for the "Fifth Week" and The Rules for Discernment

This retreat is just about over, so now is a good time to ask where we go from here. Whole books have been written on the "Fifth Week," that is, the time after the retreat formally ends. We have walked the spiritual path first outlined by Ignatius Loyola for a while. We may well have had a new spiritual awakening, perhaps even a dramatic one like Bill W.'s. What message will we carry, and what principles will we practice in all our affairs, as we re-enter "the stream of life" (BB, 86)?

We will probably want to continue with the maintenance Steps: Ten, Eleven, and Twelve. These commit us, among other things, to the "interesting and profitable . . . habit of accurate self-appraisal" (12 X 12, 89). An excellent Ignatian spiritual tool with which to attain "accurate self-appraisal" is discernment. A word of caution, however: this tool is best used by a skilled craftsman attentively and objectively listening to someone else's story. To practice discernment on yourself is as problematic as performing dentistry on yourself, and for the same reason: lack of objectivity.

The Rules for Discernment (like the entire Spiritual Exercises, in fact) are preferably to be read only by spiritual mentors and sponsors. They in turn use them to guide retreatants or sponsees. It's a bit like a sponsor getting hints from the 12 X 12 to help the sponsor in guiding a newcomer through the 12 Steps. Sponsees might well find the 12 X 12 baffling, particularly if they aren't even familiar with the Big Book, which is more basic. In the same way, retreatants might be confused or disturbed by the Rules for Discernment. Accordingly, I have buried some thoughts on the Rules for Discernment in Appendix A; the meditation for this Week will focus instead on "the interesting and profitable habit . . . of self-appraisal."

Let me suggest for your meditation this week some prayerful writing in preparation for your "Fifth Week" that you can later discuss with your spiritual guide/sponsor. As you look back over this year of meditation, what stands out for you? During which parts of the retreat did you experience the most intense feelings and desires? This will include positive and negative feelings, enthusiasm as well as repugnance (for the purposes of discernment, both are significant). What have you experienced of both? How did these strong feelings affect the life-choices you have made or reformulated? Do the feelings tell a kind of story? For example, did you begin with distaste and move on to joy? Or the other way around? What are you feeling now, near the end of the retreat? And where do you go from here?

As in 12 Step writing, be sure to ask God to be with you as you reflect and write about your retreat experience. And even if you have gotten this far without a director, you might want to pray this week that God would help you to find one, especially to read over this writing with you and discern what God is trying to tell you in it. Think of it as a kind of 5th Step.

Second Prelude, to Go: Dear God, help me to look back on the road, so I can see how far I've come, and so I can see where to direct my steps next.

Meditation 52

Last Thoughts on the Kingdom and Rules for Thinking with the Church

In this final Meditation, I suggest that you consider what has turned out to be the theme of this retreat: the Kingdom of Christ. You've spent a lot of time pondering this vision of human and divine community. Is there anywhere in your world where that vision is realized, however imperfectly? In addition, if you have made it this far in this book, you have come to know and love Jesus in a deeper way, and have made a deeper commitment to serve as he served. Is there someplace where you can channel that desire to serve? Where can you find "the fellowship you crave" (BB, 164)?

Some people find this fellowship in one of the great Christian church communities, with their rich traditions of worship and spiritual teaching. Ignatius did; after some floundering, he found the fellowship he craved among some fellow Roman Catholics whom he had directed in his Exercises. He includes some tips in the final form of the Exercises (the Rules for Thinking with the Church) about how to be a good member of this fellowship, tips representative of his views as a Roman Catholic of a particular historical epoch. I have included some thoughts on these Rules in Appendix B, for those who find this tradition congenial.

Of course, from the Twelve-Step point of view, "We think it no concern of ours what religious bodies our members identify themselves with as individuals. This should be an entirely personal affair which each one decides for him [or her] self in the light of past associations, or [their] present choices" (BB, 28). A lot of 12-Steppers, in fact, find all the fellowship they want in the 12 Step groups. As members of these groups, of course, they, too, can "be granted a glimpse of that ultimate reality which is God's kingdom" (12 X 12, 98).

Whether you find glimpses of the Kingdom in a church, with the congregation, or in the church basement, with the 12-Steppers, you can meditate with profit on how these different groups live out the call to the Kingdom. For his part, Ignatius provides Rules for "Thinking with" – or, in a better translation, "feeling with" or "sharing the attitude of" [*sentido*] – the Church. And on his side, Bill W. gave the 12 Step Groups the 12 Traditions. For your prayer this week, please take a look at these Traditions. How can you "feel with" or "share the attitude of" the 12 Traditions? I think you will see that the "attitude" of the Traditions is not far from the "attitude" of Jesus (see Phil 2:5 ff.), who came to live with us in order to serve us.

I offer a few reflections on some of the Traditions:

Tradition One – as followers of Christ, we are willing to sacrifice personal needs so that the group can continue to help people, as Jesus laid down his life so the human race could begin to recover from its addiction to violence.

Tradition Two – the only authority in our group is a loving God. As Jesus stressed at the Last Supper, leaders [in his kingdom] serve others.

Tradition Three – membership is inclusive, not exclusive. Just so, Jesus reached out by preference to untouchable people.

Tradition Five – the primary purpose of Christians, like Jesus' primary purpose, is to carry the message: the message of the Kingdom.

Tradition Six – spiritual fellowships should be radically poor. We are not "dependent upon people," or upon "money, property, or prestige"; we are "dependent upon our relationship with God" (BB, 99-100), just as Jesus was, from first to last.

Tradition Nine – 12 Step groups should have service boards, not structures, so that people can use their gifts; again, Jesus saw leadership as service, not the wielding of power.

Traditions Eleven and Twelve – 12-Steppers shouldn't bully people into recovery, and should remember to stay anonymous, for a spiritual reason: the gift of recovery is given us to give to others, not because we have special qualities or a special name. Grace is available to all the children of God, whoever they are. Jesus too used "attraction rather than promotion" in announcing the kingdom: when two disciples suggested that he should send fire down on some people who had balked at his message, he told the disciples to lighten up (Lk 9:55). And Jesus died, not just anonymous, but the willing victim of a mean joke: Pilate sarcastically captioned him "The King of the Jews" (Jn 19:19-22). Of course, the joke is forever on Pilate, because Jesus truly is a king – a king who knows that "true ambition is not what we thought it was. True ambition is the deep desire to live usefully and walk humbly under the grace of God" (12 X 12, 12:4-5; cf. Micah 6:8).

Second Prelude, to Go: Dear God, grant that I may live usefully and walk humbly under your grace, all the days of my life.

Litany of Humility

by
Rafael Cardinal Merry del Val

O Jesus! Meek and humble of heart, **Hear me.**
From the desire of being esteemed,

Deliver me, Jesus.

From the desire of being loved...
From the desire of being extolled...
From the desire of being honored...
From the desire of being praised...
From the desire of being preferred to others...
From the desire of being consulted...
From the desire of being approved...
From the fear of being humiliated...
From the fear of being despised...
From the fear of suffering rebukes...
From the fear of being calumniated...
From the fear of being forgotten...
From the fear of being ridiculed...
From the fear of being wronged...
From the fear of being suspected...
That others may be loved more than I,

Jesus, grant me the grace to desire it.

That others may be esteemed more than I...
That in the opinion of the world, others may increase and
     I may decrease...
That others may be chosen and I set aside...
That others may be praised and I unnoticed...
That others may be preferred to me in everything...
That others may be holier than I, provided that I may
     become as holy as I should...

The Serenity Prayer

by
Reinhold Niebuhr

God, grant me the serenity to accept the things I cannot change, the courage to change the things I can, and the wisdom to know the difference. Living one day at a time; enjoying one moment at a time; accepting hardship as the pathway to peace. Taking, as He did, this sinful world as it is not as I would have it. Trusting that He will make all things right if I surrender to His will. That I may be reasonably happy in this life. And supremely happy with Him forever in the next.

✛

Epilogue

You are entering on the "Fifth Week." You may wish to consult some books devoted to this topic; your director may have some ideas as well. And I have offered a few tips over the last few meditations. But in general a good guide here is the Twelfth Step: "Having had a spiritual awakening as the result of these steps [or these Exercises], we tried to carry this message to alcoholics [Al-Anon says "others" here], and to practice these principles in all our affairs" (BB, 60).

Whatever you do, don't forget the advice given by Bill W., advice enshrined in the title of the official A.A. biography of Bill (and cited above in Meditation 38): when a woman asked him how she could thank him for her recovery, he replied, "Pass it on." Promise me that you will tell the story of what happened to you during the course of this retreat to people who can profit by it. And don't forget to tell me, if you can – I love stories, thank God.

Reflections on the Rules for Discernment – For Sponsors and Directors ONLY

A Twelve-Step friend of mine, John C., read a book on Ignatian spirituality, and was thoroughly confused by the section on discernment. In fact he urged me to write something to clarify this concept, which to him "sound[ed] mysterious and remote, something like Einstein's theory of relativity or a proposition in nuclear physics. It isn't at all. Let's look at how practical it actually is" (12 X 12, 35).

Ignatius got the idea of discernment from his own spiritual experience. As I mentioned in my introduction to this book, during the earliest phase of his conversion, Ignatius did some "self-appraisal" (see 12 X 12, 89, on Step Ten), partly because there was no one he could really talk to about the spiritual changes he was going through while convalescing at his sister's castle. And he was struck by a psychological and emotional pattern that was emerging in his prayer and meditation. When he thought about making a life-choice that would entail business-as-usual, he was very happy at first, but eventually felt bored and depressed. However, when he thought about making a sweeping change in his life, about going down a completely different road – the road of spiritual progress – he was excited at first *and* he stayed excited. As he comments in his *Autobiography*, dictated many years later when he had founded the Jesuits on the principles contained in his Spiritual Exercises, this psychological insight was the beginning of his fascination with discernment. Discernment is a way to interpret our desires and feelings so as to figure out God's will for us.

It is crucial to remember that Ignatius reached the verge of suicide by trying to practice discernment on himself. His life and his sanity were literally saved when he found a good spiritual director who had enough wisdom and experience to do the discerning and to tell Ignatius what to do – primarily to stop using self-will in order to get holy in a hurry (cf. BB, 62). This kind of rookie mistake is well-attested on the Twelve-Step path as well: "Being still inexperienced and having just made conscious contact with God, it is not probable that we are going to be inspired at all times. We might pay for this presumption in all sorts of absurd actions and ideas" (BB, 87). Or even more to the point, Bill describes "a particularly disconcerting individual . . . who tries to run his [or her] life rigidly" by prayer mingled with "well-intentioned unconscious rationalizations. . . . With the best of intentions, [such persons] tend to force [their] own will[s] into all sorts of situations and problems with the comfortable assurance that [they are] acting under God's specific direction" (12 X 12, 103-4).

Bill offers the same solution as Ignatius does for such problems: Bill remarks that modern psychology agrees with the "very ancient . . . practice . . . of all spiritually centered and truly religious people" of discussing their "personality flaws . . . with an understanding and trustworthy person," in order to get "practical insight and knowledge" of where they are on their spiritual journeys (12 X 2, 56). These "spiritually centered" guides will employ several tools, and discernment can usefully be one of them.

Surely discernment was one of "the simple kit of spiritual tools" (BB, 25) that Fr. Eddie Dowling, S.J., employed in his twenty-year spiritual guidance of Bill W.

How does it work exactly? Ignatius provides two sets of Rules for Discernment. The principal difference between the two is that the first set applies mainly to people who are at present in the grip of an attachment or an addiction (SE, #313-327). Psychologically, such people tend to be in turmoil; they want to stop, but they also want to keep doing or having whatever or whomever they are addicted to. At this stage there will often be a lot of denial that there even is a problem. As a result, God's working on the person will be like an intervention – loving, but firm: "I care about you, but I want you to see how your addiction is shutting you 'off from the sunlight of the Spirit'" (cf. BB, 66).

The second set of Rules (SE, #328-336) is typically more appropriate for people who have made "the change in [their] attitude which permits [them], with humility as [their] guide, to move out from [them]selves toward others and toward God" (12 X 12, 76, on the Seventh Step). People who have gotten to this stage are likely to have gained "some measure of release from [their] more devastating handicaps" and to have found "something like real peace of mind" (12 X 12, 74). Such people "have ceased fighting anything or anyone – even alcohol" (BB, 84). Even themselves. Even God.

A common mistake that people make, especially if their practice of discernment is do-it-yourself, is to assume that, once they enter recovery, they need never use the first set of Rules again, since they are only for "spiritual beginners." I'm afraid it doesn't work that way; the usual experience of people who come to terms with Addiction A is that their Attacher simply moves over to Addiction B, and so on. Even worse, some character defects will rise up even when we think we've buried them for good.

Bill W. offers sound advice: "We need not be discouraged when we fall into the error of our old ways, for these disciplines are not easy. We shall look for progress, not perfection" (12 X 12, 91; he is of course quoting himself, BB, 60). My concise friend Terry R. says the same thing: when you enter recovery, "Don't expect to get over much." On our good days we – or our sponsors – can use the second set of Rules; on our crazy days, we and they can use the first set. On our good-and-crazy days we should probably just stick to the Serenity Prayer. And good and crazy days come the way of both newcomers and old-timers.

Ignatius also notes that, when we're in a good place, which he calls "consolation," we shouldn't get lost "in the world of spiritual make-believe" (BB, 130). Times are coming when we will learn afresh that "pain [is] the touchstone of all spiritual progress" (12 X 12, 93-4). On the other hand, when we're in a hard place, which he calls "desolation" – a word that connotes "desert," "wasteland," "loneliness" – "we should not think too ill of ourselves. . . . [Instead, we should do] what we know to be good for us," and wait for better times (12 X 12, 105). The hard times may be necessary for greater humility and honesty to break in. In any case, consolation will alternate with desolation, whether we have been in recovery 30 days or 30 years; so have your spirit-guide keep both sets of Rules close to hand.

Appendix B

Rules for Thinking with the Church

Ignatius lived, was converted, and wrote up the insights he derived from that conversion, at a very particular historical time, a time of great religious ferment (see SE, #369; Ignatius' "dangerous times," the 1500s, were like the 1930s, when the Twelve Steps evolved). While he was convalescing at his sister's castle in Spain, Northern Europe was being convulsed by the religious and political events of the Protestant Reformation. In fact, early in Ignatius' spiritual journey he was strongly suspected by local church authority – the notorious Inquisition – of having Protestant "tendencies," since he put such a premium on personal experience.

This is one reason why he includes these Rules in the Exercises (SE, #352-370). He wanted to assure his fellow Catholics that "Those having religious affiliations will find [in the Exercises] nothing disturbing to their beliefs or ceremonies" (BB, 28). I do not suggest that you read these Rules, even if you are a Roman Catholic. They are very much an artifact of their historical epoch, and some of them will seem odd or obscure in the light of the reforms introduced into Catholicism by the Second Vatican Council, called by Pope John XXIII in 1962. But I do want to underscore some principles which I think are involved in wanting to "feel with" (a better translation of "*sentir*" than "think with") a particular Christian community, a church.

The first, and most important, reason for joining a community is that we need companions on the spiritual journey. Going it alone in such matters, without companions or at the very least an individual guide, is very dangerous, as both Ignatius and Bill W. insist. But the second reason is no small matter, either: church fellowships can provide liturgical experience, the joy and comfort of ritual, whether this is as elaborate as the services of the Orthodox Churches or as simple and egalitarian as the meetings of the Society of Friends (the Quakers). Ancient rituals can be a great comfort at times of life-passages – birth, growing up, marrying, dying. I have often thought that there was a hunger for such rites and symbols in the world of the Twelve Steps, a hunger only partly fed by potlucks and anniversary coins and meeting formats.

Finally, membership in a church can be a great help in following Jesus. But of course you will want to "think" and "feel" with your church about who Jesus is and what message he carries. This is not perhaps as much a matter of theological fine points as it is of the behavior of the members. They say in A.A. that the members may be the only Big Book an active alcoholic ever sees. In the same way, church members should be studied to see if they are walking New Testaments. If the Jesus you pray to in private seems to be incarnated in a particular group of church folks, both when they worship and when they play, you might just be home.